I G S T

A PERSONAL OPERATING SYSTEM
FOR HIGH PERFORMANCE

LUKE FLOYD

TABLE OF CONTENTS

This book is dedicated to my beautiful wife,
Robin, with whom I am so privileged to journey.
Thank you for making this possible.

PREFACE

Later in my military career, I was "volun-told" to be the marksmanship trainer for my company. We had to qualify on our weapons at least annually, and in our unit, we went to the range roughly every six months. Before each qualification session, everyone had to attend a "basics" class on how to shoot, where we'd go over range orientation, the basics of marksmanship, and a safety brief.

Don't worry - you haven't accidentally received a book about marksmanship, but allow me to share a story from that experience.

New incoming privates from basic training, those who failed previous qualification attempts, or those lacking confidence would receive additional training. Each time we went to the range, which was twice a year, I conducted these remediation sessions.

Through that experience, I realized that how people feel about what they're doing directly affects their performance. For example, there was one private—we'll call him Private German—who had previously done well in marksmanship but was struggling this time. He was only hitting about 20% of the targets, which is 8 out of 40.

I pulled him off the line, sat next to him, and asked what was going on. He opened up about the tumultuous relationship he was in and the fight he had with his girlfriend before coming to that weekend's reserve training. I then sat him down and had an adult conversation about how to endure difficult situations and still perform reputably. I told him, "Imagine that stress, frustration, and pain all being put into a box. Now close that box and put it in your garage. You can return to it later. For now, you need to be present here at the range for your safety and to ensure you are set up for an eventual promotion."

He agreed, seeming to lighten at the thought of setting aside his emotional load, even if just temporarily.

"Do you believe that qualification attempt was representative of your abilities?" I asked him bluntly.

"No, Sergeant."

"Good, you're right."

With his focus returned, I walked him through the basics of marksmanship, using a system I'd developed called **PBS: Position, Breathing, Squeeze.** This system outlines the order of operations that make good marksmanship possible.

First, Position - Ensure your position is as supported as possible. You want to be a vise against as much of the ground as you're allowed in each position (prone supported, prone unsupported, kneeling). Wrench the butt end of the weapon into your shoulder, feeling fleshy contact—bone on bone causes slipping and swaying, but flesh to flesh solidifies contact.

To judge their position, I'd have them get a good sight picture (hold the sights on the center mass of the target), then close their eyes for 5 seconds and breathe deeply. If, upon opening their eyes, the sight picture had shifted, they needed to adjust their body position or support themselves with bones and body rather than holding the position with muscle. Holding yourself in position via muscles causes shaking and a lack of steadiness over even a few seconds.

If the sight picture had moved above the target, we'd shift their center of mass or hips up a couple of inches, which would drop the barrel. If it was too low, they'd shift back a few inches. They did this until their sight picture didn't change between eyes open and eyes closed.

Second, Breathing - Understand your breathing, when you're breathing in, and when you're breathing out. The timing of your breath impacts accuracy and grouping. Shots taken at mid-breath fly differently than those taken at the top or bottom of your breath. For example, if shooting three shots produced two holes at the top of the target and one at the bottom, chances are the breathing was different for the flier shot.

When I returned from Iraq and sought treatment at the VA for PTSD, one of the tools they equipped me with was box breathing, so, I incorporated it as the drill/check for this part of the system. Box breathing was simply breathing in for a four-count, hold for four, out for four. I didn't learn until later that by practicing this, we were also performing a "reset" on the autonomic nervous system. This practice was what helped me assess my own breathing patterns and become aware of them for the first time.

Third, Squeeze - You shouldn't really squeeze the trigger at all. Instead, gently pull back on the trigger until it fires. After firing, slowly release until you hear the audible click of the trigger reset, but don't fully release. This method reduces tension in the trigger, making subsequent shots less prone to being "fliers."

Again, I don't intend this to be a marksmanship book, but it's important to see how small, intentional systems can make a huge impact on performance.

I had learned these principles from my pre-deployment training before Iraq. The trainers essentially told us, "Forget what you learned in basic training, let's actually learn to shoot." They taught us about the physics behind bullets—trajectory, drag, zeroing distance, MOI, and using optics. It was almost two weeks of intense manual and mental training, re-learning to shoot as an individual.

But I distilled it down into a repeatable, digestible format that I taught as the Company PMI (Preliminary Marksmanship Instructor) to help shooters imagine—not just visualize—what they were doing. Imagine seeing the target, feeling the trigger, centering your breathing, and sensing the rifle fire. Then, slowly reset the trigger—a successful shot.

Ultimately, this led to our company leading the battalion with a 98% qualification rate on primary weapons. Once the soldiers going through the training had a system to adopt, they had a place to focus their minds.

I share this story to say we're all capable of far more than we realize. Seeing soldiers come to the range with pre-conceived, limiting beliefs about their abilities and watching those beliefs get smashed by qualifying higher than they ever had, showed me that I could help equip others with systems that elevate their performance. Achievement—making progress on or towards the completion of a meaningful activity—happens biochemically through mind maps. Circuits are created for thought in our brain based on projection and past experience.[1]

Even if you have no experience handling a firearm or only the basic training, walking up to the firing line to zero and qualify is less daunting if you have a system to focus your mind on ahead of time. The soldiers weren't trying to qualify; they were trying to execute each step of the marksmanship system to the best of their abilities, which resulted in qualification and high marks.

This experience is a perfect example of how the IGST framework can be applied in real life. My primary **intention** as

1   Dweck, C. S. (2006). *Mindset: The New Psychology of Success*. Random House. p. 16.

a marksmanship trainer was to ensure that every soldier in my company could qualify with their weapons, regardless of their previous performance or personal challenges. This intent wasn't just about passing a test—it was about building confidence, instilling discipline, and ultimately preparing these soldiers to perform under pressure in real-world situations. As you will learn later in this book, this is the first step in the IGST framework: having a clear, purposeful intent that drives everything else.

The **goal** was specific and measurable: achieve a high qualification rate for the company, ideally surpassing previous benchmarks. For each soldier, the goal was to qualify, and ideally to improve upon their previous performance. My role was to set these goals, make them clear, and help the soldiers break them down into achievable steps. Setting clear, attainable goals gives direction to your efforts.

In this scenario, the goals were tied directly to performance metrics on the firing range. By focusing on specific targets—literally and figuratively—the soldiers were able to see progress and build confidence because clear goals provide the milestones on the path to success.

The **strategy** I employed was to provide a structured system – PBS: Position, Breathing, Squeeze. This system provided a clear, repeatable process that the soldiers could rely on every time they approached the firing line. The structured training sessions, the remediation classes, and the step-by-step approach to marksmanship all provided a solid framework for them to succeed. This strategy was designed to simplify the complexities of marksmanship, making it more approachable and repeatable for every soldier, therefore, allowing them to perform consistently under pressure.

A good strategy supports consistency, which is key to mastering any skill. When you have a reliable system in place, you can execute with confidence, knowing that you're following a proven process.

Finally, the **tactics** were the specific actions I took to ensure success on the range. This included everything from individual coaching sessions, like pulling Private German aside to address his personal concerns, guiding him through PBS step-by-step, and reinforcing the importance of mental clarity during qualification. These tactics were all aligned with the broader strategy of using a systematic approach to elevate performance, ensuring that each soldier had the tools they needed to succeed.

In other words, tactics are the on-the-ground actions that implement your strategy and move you closer to your goals. Whether it's coaching a soldier through a tough moment or teaching them how to control their breathing. In the IGST framework, tactics are where the rubber meets the road—they're the actions you take to execute your plan effectively.

IGST is my life system. It is the personal operating system I use to be my very best self in every facet of my life. I'm sharing this with you as an expression of gratitude for the tools I've acquired along my journey, in hopes that you might find it useful too. Some places and names have been changed to protect identities.

Use it as a system. That's really all it is at its core. As such, adopt it at your discretion and according to your circumstances. I am not a human performance expert, so I'm not comfortable making sweeping claims about the potential of this operating system for you specifically.

I am only sharing my experience of building, implementing, and using this personal operating system to be my best self. Our actions echo through eternity, ripples in four dimensions. May this system help you amplify your ripple.

INTRODUCTION

"Oh, how blessed young men are who have to struggle for a foundation and beginning in life."
John D. Rockefeller

You're probably familiar with the chest-tightening feeling of having no, or few, choices and no safety net to catch you if you failed.

That was my reality for many years. Growing up, my family moved from Georgia to Idaho as professed "church-planter" missionaries, and I joined in tow. In high school, I had only two AP courses to choose from. I enjoyed debate and won a scholarship for it, but the college team only supported one format of the activity. A few years later, I joined the Army, walked into a reserve/guard recruiting office, and had only one option for a combat arms job. When I sought to break into software sales, I had just one friend in the industry.

I certainly had some choices, but my choices were always limited, thereby increasing the pressure to succeed exponentially. Coming from a background of socioeconomic constraints, rural upbringing, and an absence of family connections, every decision felt like a high-stakes gamble with my future as I strived to avoid being yet another statistic in the global census. Ultimately, it helped me become an exceptional problem solver.

But what if this constant feeling of being trapped was meant to be a blessing in disguise?

Initially, I fought this different perspective. I tried to mold myself according to the principles in the "sales" books; ask better questions, "close" with the right words, and build so many deals in your pipeline you couldn't possibly miss your number. This felt like a soul-sucking performance. Those books and principles might work for some individuals, but they were not the right fit for my growth and improvement. This resulted in spending years of my sales career constantly overwhelmed by the feeling of imbalance and incompetence, and being stuck on a self-worth rollercoaster tied to the sales quota attainment.

Enough

Eventually, I decided to stop fighting it and just embrace my distinct approach. What if the hardships I endured were a blessing in disguise, teaching me invaluable lessons? What if my unique worldview was my greatest asset? What if I could create solutions where I had limited choices and stop living with my back against the wall?

So, I decided to create my own path. It was time to do things *my* way. However, for me to feel comfortable and confident in this decision, I needed to test its efficacy — as proof that I wasn't just taking the "easy way out". Proof that it was possible to build a physically and financially sustainable sales career and still enjoy an early retirement.

This quest for proof sparked a year-long journey of reading, researching, networking, and being in the company of high-quality individuals and ideas that were accessible to me. I reset my sales knowledge, transformed my approach to work, and how I showed up in my personal relationships. I became ruthless with my consumption of information, making sure I only consumed content from salespeople who had carried a bag and commanded outstanding results, not self-proclaimed gurus with dubious credentials. I invested in a sales coach and joined a tight-knit community of driven professionals who were on a similar path. I developed new habits—journaling, therapy, and exercise—that helped me understand and harness my unique perspective.

The result wasn't expertise—I'm no expert. The result was a deeply authentic way of being that allowed me to be my true self and do work that felt fulfilling. This authenticity made success inevitable. I've exceeded sales quotas in seven out of eight years, earned top marks as a leader in the Army, and strengthened my relationship with my wonderful wife.

This book isn't about "best practices" or becoming a sales guru. I'm not an expert or the final say on all things sales. But I share my method, as a fellow practitioner, so you can build a unique

personal operating system for high performance in your role as a salesperson. Imagine aligning your intentions, goals, strategies, and tactics. Imagine feeling fulfilled by your work and achieving outstanding results.

This also isn't just for salespeople. The function of this operating system is to bridge multiple dimensions of life; the intentions we embody, the head goals we set, the strategies we curate, and the tactics we iterate. Anyone who is in the pursuit of achievement could take these principles and underlying research to build their own operating system for high performance, whatever that end might be.

The knowledge I'm sharing is earned. Unfortunately, you cannot take away the quick quotes or shortcut the process. In order to be effective, this book requires experiential learning. You must implement the operating system in a way that aligns with you. That takes time and dedication; this is just the primer for you to build your own system in a way that aligns your life.

That's what this book offers. It's the science, the theory, and the actionable steps to create your personal success formula. The feeling of being trapped ends as you consume and apply the content of this book. It's time to design a life with options.

CHAPTER 1:

THE JOURNEY

*"We illuminate, or darken, our lives by
the concepts we hold of ourselves."*
- Neville Goddard

Everything that is built to last has a strong foundation, and yes, this principle also applies to your career. Contrary to what you read on social media or hear in the news, success is not something you discover by chance; it's something you build intentionally. This is why it's essential to create a system.

However, individual perceptions of success may differ, but the truth remains successful individuals follow the same principle to attain success. In other words, they followed a system to attain such outstanding results. The only difference between the successful and unsuccessful is that they have not been exposed to a system of success.

Like every other unsuccessful salesperson, I was not given the "trade secrets" or any system to help me achieve success. So, what did I do? I created my own system. I won't be gatekeeping, so in this book, I will reveal the systems you need to know to get you from point A to point Z. Firstly, I want you to understand the foundation of this system through my journey as a salesperson. It all started with my bare knuckles rapping against doors.

Knock, knock.

"Hello, I'm the bug guy servicing a few of your neighbors in the area. They've noticed—"

Before I could finish my sentence, he stormed past me, <u>off his stoop</u>, and headed out to his front yard. I followed behind him, thinking he wanted us to chat in the yard. Before I realized, he bent down and picked up his water hose. Moments later, I was drenched, standing on the sidewalk as he yelled, "YOU SALES-PEOPLE ARE ALWAYS KNOCKING AT MY DOOR!"

Soaked but undeterred, I muttered, "Hey man, I'm just a college kid trying to pay bills. Sorry I interrupted you," and kept walking. Door-to-door sales was a brutal gig, but I took it one day at a time. As I approached his neighbor's house, I rang the doorbell and waited, dripping wet. The neighbor opened the door, glanced at my soaked shorts, and chuckled. Perhaps this scene was familiar to him.

"Hey, sorry for the appearance. Your neighbor sprayed me down pretty well. Do you think I said something wrong, or is he just like that?"

With a laugh, the neighbor replied, "That's not surprising. He's just like that."

"Glad it's not just me! Anyway, I'm servicing a few neighbors in the area…"

As you can see, my induction into sales wasn't glamorous. It was a summer spent dodging the hoses of grumpy clients and skeptical stares as a college kid hawking pest control. Certainly, I got soaked, but that first taste of rejection also instilled tenacity in me, which became essential on my journey. Even in the face of "No's," I was able to motivate myself to keep moving forward. But how did I get here? Let me take you back to where it all began.

With my personal life in upheaval and a mountain of bills to pay, I was drawn to a manager who visited our college campus in Idaho, recruiting college kids for a summer in sunny Florida, promising $60,000 if we worked hard and followed their system. To a college kid with student loans to pay off, this $60,000 sounded like a dream come true. The recruiter didn't even have to say it twice; I was fully committed. He repeated, "Work hard and follow our system, and you could make $60,000."

I didn't.

Well, I put in the hard work, and I strictly followed their system, but the $60,000 remained an unrealized dream. But even though this didn't seem like a positive experience, I got something much more valuable than money in the process. I learned to embrace my true identity with tenacity and finished the summer with just enough money to pay the bills and return to Idaho.

Personally, that was a major success. However, after this experience, I resigned and swore off sales completely. I didn't want to get sprayed down or interrupt people's days ever again. Just because I learned how to be tenacious doesn't mean I was comfortable with the brutal rejections of the sales industry.

An interesting fact about life is that it doesn't always go as planned. Your journey might have some short or long detours that may redirect you from the very thing you aspire to. Heck, sometimes you may feel the urge to give up on that big dream because it's too difficult, but I've realized that no matter how long it takes or how far you detour, you will always reconnect to your purpose.

A few years after my frustrating encounter with sales, I enlisted into the army and was deployed to Iraq. One would think this was my life's new trajectory, but that was not the case. After my deployment, I returned to school and focused on my passion for debate. I planned to obtain my PhD and become a professor and debate coach at a college program. This was my plan, but of course, life went in a different direction.

When my girlfriend (now my wife) and I moved in together, the mountain of bills hit me like a ton of bricks. Could I really afford another six or seven years of school just to earn an academic salary? I couldn't afford it back then, and certainly not in today's economy. I had to pivot and find a way to make ends meet, so I started looking for other job opportunities.

As I earnestly searched, I received a call for an interview with a life insurance company. 'Sales, again!' I thought. As you can imagine, I wasn't interested. Memories of my early experience in sales vividly rushed through my mind, but my girlfriend encouraged me to give the company a chance. So, I returned the call and scheduled an interview, and before I realized it, I was back in the sales game. Just like last time, this role was 100% commission, reciting a script created by someone in a B2C (business-to-consumer) environment.

Because my girlfriend and I had just gotten engaged, and my family situation had changed in the background, I committed myself entirely to succeed in my new role. I was willing to do whatever it took to make it work.

I invested a great deal of effort, and after a year, I had already traveled 40,000 miles, saved up a few thousand dollars in the bank, and achieved President's Club and two promotions. This was technically a "successful" year. But I wanted out. The B2C industry was being heavily disrupted by technology, and I saw the writing on the wall. I knew that very soon, there would be an oversaturation of insurance agents, making the market even more competitive than it already was, and would probably go the way of the dodo bird.

The silver lining was the gift that this role afforded me called "windshield time." As it turns out, those 40,000 miles were enough time to listen to audiobooks, think, and plan. One fateful day in 2015, I listened to a program on the NPR station, to which my radio was permanently affixed, about the world of tech sales. This was an entirely different sector from what I was used to - working at a big company with big companies to help them adopt new software and technology. The program even claimed the salespeople were earning more than some doctors and lawyers – $300,000 or $400,000 and beyond - each year.

A light went off in my head—'I need to get into that world,' I thought. I researched furiously, revamped my LinkedIn, and reconnected with a friend from school who was in the SaaS (Software as a Service) industry for businesses selling to other businesses. He was a tech salesperson working with a CRM management agency and also had a startup in-house. After a short interview, I started a new job as a Business Development Representative for his group.

I was ecstatic. I could sit at a computer all day instead of speeding through multiple appointments as I did in my previous job, trading a computer screen for the windshield. I got to make cold phone calls instead of going to properties in rural Georgia. I could speak with executives and business people who I couldn't access previously. And I got paid a base salary? This was thrilling and I was all in.

Eventually, I got "promoted" to an account executive role, then another promotion into an AE role with a better compensation plan, and then realized I was pretty tired of sales. My existence was chained to my number; if I was crushing it, I was on top of the world, but if I was missing quota, it was end-of-month tension headaches.

This wasn't a good way to live.

Due to my success in building healthy relationships with some of my colleagues and channel partners in my role as Account Executive at Granular, I was offered a role to move up into the corporate parent company, basically doing indirect channel sales enablement.

This role dealt with farmers and the agricultural economy eco-system around them, from the Mississippi Delta in the west to the Atlantic Ocean in the east. It was a nascent opportunity with little support; I was required to travel often (50% of the time), and the parent company had just undergone a merger. It was a tough gig, but growing up with little means, when they offered a six-figure salary and a company truck it was a no-brainer. Plus, the classic direct sales roles had weighed on me mentally, and I felt like I could use a change of pace.

This role was a game-changer for two reasons:

1. **Autonomy**: I had little to no supervision. This was a "big boy" corporate job, reporting to higher-level supervisors who didn't impose strict management on my activities. Since the efforts in the region were still new, I was asked to build our go-to-market plan, including my personal goals. This was an

entirely different way to work compared to the micromanaging world of SaaS sales.

2. **Windshield time**: I spent hundreds of hours on the road. I put the company truck to use doing a constant roadshow of farm visits, corporate training, retail visits, and "field days."

These two blessings in disguise would prove to change my life.

The first blessing gave me the freedom to exercise extreme ownership, as it was at that time I read the book *Extreme Ownership* by Jocko Willink[2], which completely upended the way I saw my job. It was like applying the parts of military leadership I enjoyed the most. Progressing from a monthly quota, which rolls up to a yearly number, to an annual number with no plan was an entirely different way of working. My success wasn't governed by the daily appointments on my calendar but by my ability to create a vision for the business unit, resource the vision appropriately, and then generate local momentum with my colleagues.

The second blessing gave me the opportunity to craft a vision for my future. Hundreds of hours of podcasts, audiobooks, conversations with friends, and just quiet gave me space to understand my aspirations and life goals. In this white space, I realized it was possible to embrace sales as a craft and have different outcomes from my previous attempts. I could do it differently this time.

---

2   Willink, J., & Babin, L. (2015). *Extreme Ownership: How U.S. Navy SEALs Lead and Win*. St. Martin's Press

Eventually, as an attribute of the corporate roles, our annual bonus was capped, and so was our income. This was a bit of a blow to me. I had gotten into sales because the rewards were proportional to the effort invested, not so I could earn the same amount as the next guy despite my extra effort. I had increased my earnings consistently for five years straight - which felt like a survival necessity coming from little means - but that trend was set to end.

So, during my windshield time, I asked myself: 'If I had the opportunity to venture into sales, but was doing it differently this time, how would I capitalize on it?'

The result was a research project akin to a graduate degree. I consumed books on performance psychology, goal setting, sales history, and process. I listened to every episode of the Sales Success Stories podcast - a long-form interview podcast with only bag-carrying, top-performing sellers - and extracted common themes. Every discussion and opportunity during my time in the corporate role became an opportunity to test and improve with my new approach.

I learned three core lessons from these experiences, and these form the basis of this book:

1. **Sales is a craft:** It rewards those who embrace it with dedication and passion. I learned this by listening to high earners like Brandon Fluharty, Jamal Reimer, and Trong Nguyen, who spoke about this.

2. **Having a system is essential:** Success requires aligning goals, strategies, and actions with core principles. Individually, "best practices" for sales aren't sufficient to attain success, as they are just tactics. A strategy needs action to make it complete. Your goals need to be motivated by higher guiding principles that resonate with your identity. This alignment could be built through an operating system.

3. **Leverage your strengths:** Success in sales is about leveraging unique strengths to help clients make the best decisions. Betting on yourself is a sure path to success.

Coincidentally, a previous manager who was leading sales at Deel (an incredibly fast-growing Global HR & Payroll startup) asked if I wanted to join their sales team targeting larger accounts. This was an opportunity to join a generational company and implement the system I had been building for years.

The cost was a pay cut to my cushy corporate base salary, giving up the sweet company truck, and getting back into the monthly quota grind. When he called to make the offer, I stubbornly told him, "Whatever number you set for my quota, I will double it."

I reached out to Scott Ingram, the host of the Sales Success Podcast, to express gratitude for how his podcast helped me find my way back into the craft, affirming that I would appear on his show as the top performer or 1% of my sales team, as this was the requirement to be a guest on his show.

Here's the catch. I bet on myself! I called the shot and claimed I would not only double but triple my earnings.

And I did!

This milestone didn't just happen by chance. It's important to emphasize that I didn't bet on myself blindly. At this point in my life, after all my hours of research, learning, and listening, I had created a fail-proof operating system for success.

I'm sharing this operating system and underpinning tools, templates, and research that led to my success, hoping they can help you achieve your vision, too. The beauty of this operating system is that it can be tailored to individual needs. So, this system will work for you whether your story is similar to mine or completely different. Let's get into it.

CHAPTER 2:

THE OPERATING SYSTEM

"You do not rise to the level of your goals. You fall to the level of your systems."
James Clear

I like to use the concept of an operating system as a heuristic for an overarching framework that governs how I structure my life. One of the essential requirements for sales is the constant focus on tips, tricks, and "how-tos" that remain purely tactical. At some point, you need a broader strategy to govern your tactics. However, what if it were possible to align your broader strategies to exist in the world with incredible goals to form an intention you can live out daily?

As humans, we are more complex than computers, which can be a helpful analogy to understand how to get your various components working together.

For example, humans have a "hardware component"—which includes your physical body and brain - made up of electrical pulses through cells. Just like with a computer, the human hardware component determines your capabilities. When Atari invented Pong, it was revolutionary for the history of video games[3]. However, when releasing the next generation of the console, 'The Atari 2600,' games could only be designed and played based on the Pong architecture because the hardware was only designed for that. Meanwhile, when Nintendo released hardware that contained a graphics card, it enabled game developers to build freely without constraint, opening up new possibilities for the "software" that could be supported by the console's hardware.

On the other hand, in our analogy, we have the "software component"—the mental thoughts and capabilities produced by our hardware. The software includes the ability to hold a specific type of business conversation to evaluate the current and future state to determine a potential partnership. Similarly, the ability to communicate via writing and build consensus through asynchronous communication is another example of software. Our habits, mental systems, and underlying belief structures are also essential parts of the "software component" that can extract the greatest potential from our hardware.

Let's break this down a little further so it's easier to digest.

---

3   Newport, C. (Host). (2023, August 7). *Episode 287: How to Organize Your Time Like a Billionaire* [Audio podcast episode]. In *Deep Questions with Cal Newport*. Spotify. https://www.calnewport.com/podcast

Hardware:
Consider your hardware as your innate capabilities – the foundation upon which you build your sales skills. This includes:

- **Your Physical Body:** Endurance, stamina, and overall health are essential for the demands of sales.
- **Your Mental Acuity:** Sharp thinking, problem-solving abilities, and the ability to learn and retain information are crucial assets.
- **Your Communication Skills:** The ability to connect with people, express yourself clearly, and build healthy relationships are key drivers of success.

Software:
Software represents the collection of tools, processes, and strategies you leverage to achieve your goals as a salesperson. Here are some key software components:

- **Sales Methodology:** A structured framework that guides you through the sales process.
- **Prospecting Techniques:** Strategies for identifying and qualifying potential leads.
- **Communication Tools:** Utilizing technology like CRM (Customer Relationship Management) software to streamline workflows and manage client interactions.
- **Sales Scripts:** Templates that provide a foundation for your sales conversations.

I'm certainly not the first person to suggest using the operating system heuristic in sales. However, at this point in my career,

I understand that the operating system I've uncovered through years of practice and research is bigger than sales. It's useful as an operating system for anyone in any field; I just happen to have used sales as the vehicle to find it.

An operating system is defined as:

- **The software that supports a computer's basic functions, such as scheduling tasks, executing applications, and controlling peripherals.**

The operating system connects the hardware and software together to make capabilities accessible. Throughout my experience across the military, sales, and other fields of life, I've encountered different types of humans: smart, dull, driven and motivated, listless, hungry, and incapable. A common trait among most individuals I've encountered is the presence of discipline amongst many. During my service in the military, I realized that almost everyone can be disciplined when subjected to the appropriate system governing identity and motivation.

Discipline is not the ability to sit down and make fifty cold calls in a row. Discipline is the ability to align motivation—your underlying inspiration, your intention—with requisite action. In this way, if you're feeling unmotivated or undisciplined because you find it hard to do the things you're "supposed" to do to be successful, you probably already possess all the skills needed to be successful but need to fuel action.

You are not deficient in skills. You possess the ability to achieve or the will to learn the necessary skills required to attain your desired goal. The inability to attain success isn't due to our lack of motivation or discipline; it's about discovering your vision and letting it fuel your alignment.

Probably, you don't need more discipline or motivation; you just need a system that aligns your hardware and software to produce incredible results in a readily accessible format. You need an operating system.

I understand why some might be hesitant to adopt a framework based on computer terminology—hardware, software, operating system. It can feel like it strips us of our humanity. But the craft of sales presents us with an opportunity to develop mastery by leaning into our humanity.

As Robert Greene lays out in *Mastery*[4] Our brain has evolved over millions of years to display key traits: the ability to read patterns, the predisposition to be social animals, and the ability to focus. Sales can be a culmination of these highest forms of our evolution. When done correctly or executed with most humanity—sales is about leaning into our ability to relate, problem solve, and our innate ability to predict and shape the future.

Acting in these ways feels right. When you get into a deep state of focus in work or play, you're rewarded with "flow"—a release of dopamine and other chemicals that reward the brain. When you solve problems, your brain rewards you again with "feel good"

---

4   Greene, R. (2012). *Mastery*. Viking Adult. p. 39.

chemicals. For more information on flow and using it to do your best work, see *The Art of Impossible* by Steven Kotler.

Your challenge in becoming the best version of yourself within the confines of the craft of sales is to embrace the natural wiring of your brain to achieve high performance. You were meant to do this; you just have to do it the right way.

This pays respect to your ancestors, which feels right. This connects you to a broader social purpose, which feels right. This taps into some unspoken intelligence we all share—the result of millions of years of neurological evolution—which feels right.

The most crucial part of crafting this operating system is to gain clarity on our guiding truth, our motto for living, and our "why," through an intention statement.

The Core Truths Underlying This Operating System

1. The stories we tell ourselves determine our reality.
    a. All physical reality is mentally interpreted and constructed.[5]
    b. Our physical biology primes our ability to interpret. That makes emotional states the filter for how we interpret the world.[6]

---

5   Kastrup, B. (2019). *The Idea of the World: A Multi-Disciplinary Argument for the Mental Nature of Reality.* Imprint Academic.
6   Barrett, L. F. (2017). *How Emotions Are Made: The Secret Life of the Brain.* Houghton Mifflin Harcourt. pp. 46-48.

    c. We can prime our emotional states.

    d. Therefore, we can affect our reality by priming our emotional states.

2. You are enough.

    a. Just as you are today.

    b. You possess the skills needed to achieve beyond what you ever thought was possible - they just need to be aligned.

3. Success in infinite games (like life and long-term professions) is determined by how well you manage limited resources.[7] Your most precious resources are those which are discrete/finite: energy, time, and focus.

    a. The motions of modern life are built upon average people not being fully conscious and present in the world. If you can consciously design your life, you can achieve your desired goal.

4. Lack of motivation or "self-discipline" is a myth. There is no inherent deficit that makes one person less "disciplined" than another. There is only a lack of alignment and motivation towards a crafted vision - when you know what you want, you will do *whatever it takes* to create it.

5. Knowledge that can be applied is the knowledge that must be earned. You cannot read this book to develop this system exactly as it is written on the page; it must be adopted through thoughtful reflection of experience and iteration.

---

7   Sinek, S. (2019). *The Infinite Game*. Portfolio/Penguin. pp. 13-16.

The Art of Optimization:
A Three-Step Approach

How do we transform our software collection from a jumbled mess into an excellent sales machine? Here's a three-step approach:

1. **Experimentation and Data-Driven Decisions:**
   - **Don't be afraid to experiment:** Treat your software like a scientist treats a hypothesis. Try out different sales methodologies, prospecting techniques, and communication styles. In other words, test your software on your hardware to find out what works best for you as an individual.
   - **Track your results:** Monitor key metrics like conversion rates, average deal size, and sales cycle length.
   - **Analyze and adapt:** Use data to identify your successes and failures. Refine your approach based on what generates the best results.

2. **Prioritize and Focus:**
   - **Not all tools are created equal:** Identify the 20% of activities that generate 80% of your results (*the Pareto Principle*).[8] The Pareto Principle, also known as the 80/20 rule, is a concept that suggests that 80% of consequences come from 20% of causes. In other words, a small number of inputs or actions are responsible for the large outputs or results we record. It's important to realize that the Pareto Principle is not a rigid mathematical principle. The exact percentages may vary depending on the situation.

---

8   Ferriss, T. (2007). *The 4-Hour Workweek: Escape 9-5, Live Anywhere, and Join the New Rich.* Crown Publishing Group. pp. 68-70.

- **Focus on mastery, not mediocrity:** Instead of spreading yourself thin across countless tactics, dedicate time to mastering the most productive strategies. For example, according to the Pareto Principle, 20% of your clients might generate 80% of your revenue. This means that you can significantly boost your bottom line by focusing on retaining and upselling to high-value clients rather than spending countless hours in an attempt to connect with subordinate clients.

3. **Regularly update your operating system:**
   - **Stay in the loop:** Stay up to date with the trends of the industry and, most importantly, the needs of your client. A fast way to guarantee a sale is to provide a solution to the needs of a client.
   - **Refine your pitch:** Personally, I detested having to read the same script hundreds of times. Now imagine how a client feels having to hear a similar script from the different salespeople who knocked on their door. I can bet the salesperson who closed the sale was the one who was "different" and offered a genuine solution to the client's changing needs.

To recap, your hardware and your software must always be in harmony for you to feel fulfilled and achieve results. This harmony must align with your vision statement. Remember, having a good tactic can easily get you the desired results, but at some point, you will hit a brick wall, and the only way around that is to return to the authenticity of your operating system.

This chapter has covered the framework of your operating system. At this point, we're going to dive deep and examine the fundamentals that form the fibers and networks of your system.

This chapter has been a review of the basic framework for your operating system, the hardware and software that makes the entire system function. Now, it's time to delve deeper and examine the fundamentals that form the fibers and networks of your system.

CHAPTER 3:

INTENTION

*"Life isn't about finding yourself,
it's about creating yourself."*
George Bernard Shaw

Intention is one of those words used liberally by individuals across many disciplines. We see its use in different motivational speeches and self-help books, and it's made to sound so easy, so formulaic, and so static! Through my journey in life, I've discovered that intention should be the furthest thing from static. Just like humans, your intention must continuously develop and transform to remain in alignment with your journey. However, you have to remain cognizant enough to change your intention statement to align with your journey.

Imagine going on a road trip without a definite destination. You might end up wandering aimlessly, making random turns, and never really reaching your full potential. An intention statement functions like the GPS for your life's journey. It provides clarity and direction and keeps you moving in the right direction so you can make the right choices daily. When you have an intention, everything else aligns because it is instrumental in the journey to fulfilling your big goal.

What is an Intention Statement?

An intention statement is a clear, present-tense declaration that captures your core purpose and desired outcomes. It's not a vague wish or a to-do list item; it's a driving force that ignites your passion and fuels your actions. It's a concise, powerful declaration that captures your "why" – your core purpose and driving motivation.[9]

Here are some key benefits of crafting a powerful intention statement:

- **Clarity:** It cuts through the noise and helps you identify what truly matters.
- **Focus:** It keeps you laser-focused on your goals and prevents distractions.
- **Motivation:** It serves as a constant source of inspiration and drive.
- **Decision-Making:** It provides a framework for evaluating opportunities and making choices aligned with your purpose.

9   Adams, J. (2019). *Intention Matters: The Science of Creating the Life You Want.* Intentional Creations.

So, how do you draft this intention statement? Let's examine four (4) simple steps:

1. **Deep Reflection:** This is an introspective journey. Conduct a self-examination and ask yourself: What are my core values? What kind of impact do I want to make? What brings me a sense of fulfillment? Take an inventory of your thoughts and feelings.

2. **Identify Your Driving Force:** What is the underlying motivation that fuels your desire for success in sales? Is it financial security for your family? Is it the thrill of the challenge? Is it the satisfaction of helping others achieve their goals? Discover the "why" behind your "what."

3. **Craft Your Statement:** Here comes the fun part! Using your identified values and motivations, write a concise and powerful statement that captures your intention. Aim for clarity, conciseness, and inspiration.

4. **Refine and Revise:** Don't settle for the first draft. Let your statement sit for a while, then revisit it with a fresh thought. Refine the language, ensuring it resonates with your identity.

Example Structure:

- "I am committed to [core values] in order to [purpose/impact], and I will achieve [specific goals] by [actions/behaviors]."

Example Statement:

- "I am committed to growth, integrity, and compassion. My purpose is to exceed all my targets and double my income. I will achieve my goal of becoming the top sales-person in my company by continuously learning, asking questions, and refining my sales techniques."

Important tips to remember:
- **Keep it Positive:** Frame your intention statement positively. Focus on your goals and not your obstacles.
- **Be Specific:** Avoid vague language. The clearer your statement, the more effective it will be.
- **Make it Personal:** Your intention statement should reflect your unique values, purpose, and goals. It should feel authentic and deeply personal.
- **Embody it:** Intentions are embodied assumptions and beliefs manifested through thought. Feel the statement - in your body - as you write or say it.

Having a toolbox full of wrenches doesn't make you a mechanic. In the same vein, possessing a vast knowledge of sales methodologies and an arsenal of communication tools isn't enough to guarantee success. The key to success lies in **optimizing your software**, in other words, transforming your knowledge into a streamlined system that empowers you to excel.

When drafting your intention statement, every word is important. Ultimately, we're talking about practical magic—focusing your energy toward the specific intent to unlock an expected outcome. It's a small prayer said daily to whoever or whatever you believe in. Each word needs to be carefully chosen because it can have unintended effects.

Additionally, your intention statement can change as you progress on your journey. This is one of the most important pieces of information that is often kept a secret. Your intention statement MUST change as you change in order to keep your operating system functioning in alignment.

Think of it this way: Imagine you apply for an entry-level job at a Fortune 500 company. Your first intention statement would be framed around striving to secure the job. Once you're in and acclimated to the system, your new goal might become a manager, a specialist, or maybe even a VP. Each of these goals would require a unique intention statement because each of these positions requires you to improve yourself to a different degree.

Let's examine a few intention statements I've cycled through in recent years:

First iteration:
"Achieve personal, professional, and financial freedom through focused and intentional sales mastery."

In this intention statement, I was primarily focused on achievement. I wanted to do 200% of the quota, regardless of what that might be. While this is laughably limiting, looking back on it, the quota has no bearing on my potential, and using it as a baseline was a disservice to my abilities. However, I had to start from somewhere. From there, I simply modified the wording as my goals or daily reflections changed.

Second Iteration:
"Achieve personal, professional, and financial freedom through focused and balanced sales excellence."

At the time, I was honed in on finding a better work/life balance. This one-word change wasn't sufficient, obviously, but it reflected my mindset at the time. As I began releasing the shackles of quota on my mindset, it morphed into:

Third iteration:
"Unlock personal, professional, and financial freedom through focused and balanced sales excellence."

This freedom—which has always been a centerpiece of my drive—was out there for me to find and unlock, not achieve. It wasn't behind some goal; it was a puzzle I was pursuing to solve daily.

At one point, I plunged into a phase of burnout due to the massive sales opportunity I was working tirelessly to close. Back then, our organization really underestimated the workload required for such large deals. This is because our processes and systems were designed for average-scale projects, and it took a lot more effort to handle this big opportunity. While I received some support, I had to fight tooth and nail for the resources I needed to keep everyone aligned, which took a significant toll on me. Thankfully, this experience wasn't in vain. Fortunately, we were able to provide feedback which prompted positive changes within the organization, with processes and systems improved and equipped to handle complex deals.

As a result of this low spot, I changed my daily intention to reflect my current phase.

Burnout phase:
"Be authentic, be present, be slow."

I retained that intention statement for about six months until I regained myself. The larger deals were on hold—I just wanted to get back to being me.

At the time of this writing, my current intention statement is reflective of how difficult the year 2023 was for my family and I. We lost four different family members, including my emotional support animal, who had been with me since I returned from Iraq. We faced sickness and re-evaluated relationships, all of which took a huge emotional toll. It felt like a crucible, which produced this intention statement:

"Forge personal, professional, and financial freedom through authentic and intentional sales excellence."

As observed in my intention statement, my aims (freedom) and my vehicle (sales excellence) have remained consistent, regardless of the phases of life. Each of the words is clearly defined:

- **Personal freedom:** means being able to express my true identity and be the person I want to be.
- **Professional freedom:** means having the skill set to work how I want to work.

- **Financial freedom:** means I want to be financially independent—not required to work as a means of survival.

This intention statement is a living, breathing presence in my life now. I write it down almost daily (every workday, some weekends). I consistently meditate on it. It's simply a vehicle to focus my energy toward a specific outcome.

Why Intention Matters

While many might consider setting your intention to be "woo-woo" or "out there," it's based on both history and science. In his classic "Think and Grow Rich," Napoleon Hill discusses this in the form of written affirmations.[10] After studying "self-made" men, he advised writing your goals daily in the form of active accomplishment. For me, this became "I have achieved 200% of my quota." The purpose of your intention statement is to channel your energy into a specific focus, therefore priming your brain to interpret and construct reality towards that focus.

Interestingly, science has supported Hill's ideas. There are several mechanisms for how intention statements might influence our reality.

---

10   Hill, N. (1937). *Think and Grow Rich*. The Ralston Society. pp. 70-72.

"Priming" Your Brain for Action

The core principle is this: channeling your energy into a specific focus primes your brain to interpret and shape your reality towards that focus. This idea relies on a few underlying principles:

1. **Selective Attention**: Our brains select what information to process. There is more information in your environment than your brain could ever process. Some of this information—the feeling of the wind in your hair, the color of the sky, the honking of a car, the numbers on the houses you pass by on your drive — is sometimes entirely disregarded and not noticed. Even our eyes, which are extensions of our brains, can only process information within certain wavelengths.

2. **Perceptual Filling-In**: Our brain "fills in" details along the way. Our brain draws on the sensory information, along with memories of previous contextually-related experience, to fill in details where the "spotlight" of our attention is not actively focused.[11]

3. **Mental Construct of Reality**: Our entire environment is a product of our mental construct. While I don't need to delve into the philosophy of Analytical Idealism from Kastrup above, there's solid philosophical, logical, and scientific proof that everything around us is an interpretation of our mind.

---

11   Jha, A. P. (2021). *Peak Mind: Find Your Focus, Own Your Attention, Invest 12 Minutes a Day*. Harper Wave. pp. 84-86.

Given these steps, it's possible for us to metaphorically set the table for observation while we prime our Reticular Activating System (RAS). The RAS is a network of neurons in the brainstem that plays a key role in attention and consciousness. It filters the vast amount of sensory information we receive, highlighting what is important and filtering out what is not. When you articulate a clear intention statement, your RAS begins to focus on information and opportunities that align with that intention. This selective attention helps you notice things that can help you achieve your goals, which you might otherwise overlook (Arguinchona & Tadi, 2023).

The human brain is incredibly adaptable, a characteristic known as neuroplasticity. Neuroplasticity refers to the ability of the human brain to reorganize itself by forming new neural connections throughout life in response to stimuli (Marzola, Melzer, Pavesi, Gil-Mohapel, & Brocardo, 2023). When you consistently focus on a specific intention, you essentially train your brain to recognize and prioritize the thoughts, actions, and opportunities that align with that intention. Repeating an intention statement reinforces these neural pathways, making it easier to act in line with your goals.

Interoception:
Feeling Your Way to Success

Interoception is defined as "the sensing of physiological signals originating inside the body."[12] This sounds like a complex scientific term, but it really isn't. To "break it down Barney-style," as commonly said in the Army, it's your ability to recognize what your body is feeling.

For example, a study was performed on financial traders in the London Stock Exchange. From the outcome of the survey, traders who were more "in touch" with their bodies performed better—this suggests that they possessed better interoceptive ability to feel their heart rate compared to control groups. The study concluded that "the interoceptive ability of traders predicted their relative profitability, and strikingly, how long they survived in the financial markets."

Here's how interoception can be combined with intention setting:

1. **Focus on Your Core Theme:** Deeply consider what you want to achieve.
2. **Body Mapping:** Identify the parts of your body where this goal evokes specific emotions (e.g., feeling of pride in your chest).
3. **Mind-Body Connection:** Observe your body and intentionally recreate those feelings throughout the day.

---

12   Kandasamy *et al.* Interoceptive Ability Predicts Survival on a London Trading Floor. Sci Rep. 2016 Sep 19;6:32986. doi: 10.1038/srep32986. PMID: 27641692; PMCID: PMC5027524.

Within some guardrails of actions beyond your control, it's possible to select feelings that generate action, prime those feelings in your RAS through a meditative or reflective practice that encourages those feelings, and then intentionally observe your body throughout your day.

I know this is possible because I've had a personal experience. When I first started at Deel, I realized I had never felt "pride" in my role as a salesperson. Maybe that was because of the connotations of being in sales; perhaps I just never stopped to analyze what I was feeling, or maybe I hadn't done any work I felt was worth being proud of yet. However, three months after I started in my role, I was deep into my daily ritual of mindfulness and consistently journaling my intentions.

In an attempt to help you visualize what interoception looks like in a practical sense, let's walk down my memory lane. I began on a Tuesday morning of work with a guided meditation that combined mindfulness with visualization. Laying on a mat in my basement office, I focused on my breathing and listened as the meditation asked me to visualize some desired achievements, something I had been aiming and striving towards.

The guide asked me to see what I was wearing, listen to the environment around me, observe the specific facial expressions of those around me, and feel—in my body, not just theoretically identifying—the feelings that arose from having achieved that accomplishment. I visualized myself in a boat on a lake, fishing with my wife, in complete peace, having taken time off work after accomplishing my quota that year. I heard the birds chirping and the gentle lapping of the reservoir against the metal frame of the boat. I smelled the crisp air of the late fall in Georgia. Then, I felt a sense of pride in having accomplished my goals as a salesperson. It was a deep, warm feeling that spread across my chest, literally lifting my chest and pushing my shoulders back. By the end of the meditation, I was in tears at how *real* it all felt.

Later that day, I had an introductory call scheduled for a prospective client who would have been a monumental win for us at the time—more than a year's worth of quota for me, specifically. Even though I was still new in my role, I wanted to handle this call myself and felt confident going into it. The call went off without a hitch; it felt like I entered a state of flow (which is possible in conversation), and I naturally guided the call and my light product demonstration through the key points I knew would earn me a second conversation. When I hopped off the call, I was buzzing with a neurochemical cocktail released from such a performance; anyone in a performance profession can resonate with that feeling. Like clockwork, though, I immediately also felt that deep, warm feeling in my chest—pride that I had executed the call so cleanly, helped my prospect in their decision-making journey, and without any overbearing help from my manager at the time.

My operating system was the perfect framework to repeatedly experience that buzzy feeling or any feeling necessary to achieve my goals. Before that day, I wasn't proud about being a salesperson, but after that experience, I did not only feel proud but discovered what it took to be consistently proud about being a salesperson.

Tools for Intention Journaling

A major part of intention-setting is writing it down. It is one of the most powerful ways of solidifying your intention. It also forces you to articulate your goals clearly. Most individuals are terrified at the thought of elevator pitches. We often fumble and bite our tongues while we try to unscramble our thoughts. Now imagine how different this scenario would be if you already had a powerful script already memorized. It would turn those two dreaded minutes in that elevator into sales heaven.

I never kept a journal just to write my thoughts in. It felt over-whelming—*did I have to write down stuff every single day?* Once I understood daily journaling as a way to better clarify my inter-nal vision and calm my mind, I was compelled to build a daily practice. I engaged in different journaling practices that proved to be very valuable. However, you don't have to do both of these practices, but I encourage you to practice at least one of the two (especially the intention and goal alignment practice).

Intention and Goal Alignment Journaling

My current journaling practice revolves around my core inten-tion and associated goals. Here are three (3) tips that can help you align your journal with your aspirations:

1. **Review Your Intention Statement:** Consistently revisit and refine your intention statement to ensure it remains relevant and aligned with your evolving life and aspirations. If you're still unable to do this, revert to the beginning of this chapter,

where I revealed the intention statements I've had over the years.

2. **Break Down Goals:** Large goals can feel overwhelming, especially when you're looking up from the bottom of your mountain. Break your goals down into smaller, more realistic steps that are achievable. For example, if your company has different rewards for different sales targets, you can pace yourself to meet each target step by step instead of shooting for the highest target at your first instance. **[Note: this doesn't mean you should dream small. No! The point is to know yourself well enough to apply what works best for you]**

3. **Daily Reflections:** Develop a habit of revisiting your intention statement and reflecting on your progress. This will reinforce your commitment and help you stay focused. This doesn't have to be a long journaling session. Even a few minutes of conducting daily reflection will make a huge difference. Remember, the goal is to turn your intention into a habit.

Dream Journaling

As I mentioned earlier, I've also engaged with dream journaling and found it valuable. Dream journaling involves writing down your dreams immediately upon waking. Unless they're captured within 60–90 seconds after waking, they can fade or be hard to remember.

I've found dream journaling to be helpful in capturing broader themes. I certainly write down the specific scenes of the dream, but what is more indicative to me—and therefore more help-ful—are the vibes. Capturing the specific feelings and emotions expressed in the dream is just another data point for better un-derstanding and aligning your internal vision.

I also try to capture specific topics or themes. For example, water often appears in my dreams, like fishing, boating, or swimming. Another topic might be having a "test" appear in the dream or having the lights turned out in a room. Between the emotions felt and the topics covered, I'm able to gather more data to an-alyze my feelings. And there's no wearable tech to analyze your dreams yet, so a daily practice of dream journaling can help build the habit of immediate reflection.

To recap, dream journaling comprises of these three (3) things:

1. **Capture the Essence:** Don't worry about perfect grammar or sentence structure. Focus on capturing the key elements of your dream, particularly the feelings and emotions they evoke.

2. **Immediate Recall:** Dreams fade quickly. Keep a pen and notebook by your bedside and write down your dreams as soon as you wake up because the details tend to fade within minutes (60 to 90 seconds).

3. **Themes and Symbols:** Over time, observe the recurring themes or symbols in your dreams. These will reveal the deeper truths of your subconscious desires or anxieties that you may not be aware of.

Sincerely, the habit of journaling is not easy to adopt. That's why you need a solid "Intention!"

Do whatever it takes to make this a habit. Even if you have to set alarms or reminders on your phone or include it in your daily itinerary, do it! The level of your success is directly proportional to your degree of intention.

Mindfulness Practice

Remember that interesting word we learned earlier called "Interoception?" A word that simply means being in tune with your body. For example, if you haven't eaten all day and you notice your stomach grumbling, or if you have an important meeting and notice a pit in your stomach or chest tightening from anxiety, that's interoception.

But the real question is: what is the connection between interoception and sales?

My input on this subject is anecdotal, but I noticed that I'm at my "sales best" when I'm most in tune with myself - my body, my mind, and my spirit.

In her book "Peak Mind,"[13] Dr. Amishi Jha outlines the benefits of having a structured mindfulness practice. One surprising bit of research she highlighted is that London stockbrokers' interoception ability predicted their relative profitability and long-term

---

13   Jha, A. P. (2021). *Peak Mind: Find Your Focus, Own Your Attention, Invest 12 Minutes a Day.* Harper Wave.

survival in the industry. Another example is a 2015 paper that argued improving mindfulness, along with decision-making, improves legal ethics and professionalism.[14]

Why Mindfulness Matters

Mindfulness isn't just a practice that makes you feel better physically or think more clearly. It can also help break down the old patterns of context which create our unconscious reactions.

When I was in Iraq, my group's broader role was Route Clearance. We had specially-equipped vehicles which could investigate, and help blunt the blasts from, IEDs - improvised explosive devices, or roadside bombs. At night, to clear the route for morning traffic, we'd drive very slowly over familiar routes, with lights blaring down onto the side of the roads, looking for anything suspicious in the routine trash and debris.

While this job was certainly harrowing at times - the goal was to find and neutralize the IED before it did the same to you or your friends - it was also incredibly pattern-based. We had a couple routes we were responsible for clearing every day so that convoys and local traffic was not at risk (IEDs were a major driver of civilian casualties). That meant five days a week, with one day spent in the motorpool maintaining our equipment and vehicles and one day spent to recover, we would drive between five and

---

14 Riskin, L. L. (2015). *Mindfulness in the Law and Legal Ethics: A Challenge for the Profession.* In *Washington University Journal of Law & Policy,* 48, 135-168.

ten miles per hour for six to eight hours at a time down the same few routes. Boring, until it wasn't.

While this makes it seem routine - rolling down the same routes, doing the same job, looking at the same trash over and over again - we also had to be ready for it to be very much not routine at a moment's notice. Whether that meant being prepared for enemy attack, finding the IEDs before they detonated on one of our trucks, or responding to the loud boom telling us the IEDs had found us first, there was this interesting balance of being absolutely tuned in to something that was routine.

"Was that box placed like that last night?" "Is that dirt lighter than its surroundings in the ditch?"

"Is that a wire running out of those trees?"

The unit I deployed with had also performed route clearance in Ramadi and Fallujah in 2006-2007 - a much different period of the Iraq war than when I deployed in 2011. While we encountered fifteen or sixteen IEDs during our nine months operating (we found some, some found us), my unit would find as many during *one night* of operations. This led my leadership to instill the attention to detail necessary to keep us as safe - at least as safe as possible.

You can imagine how keeping your nervous system tuned up for complete awareness, while encountering the same things over and over, might produce a default state of arousal.

Others didn't do their job in the same way, however.

Towards the end of our deployment, we spent a month in Kirkuk in the northern part of Iraq. We took over for an active duty route clearance unit who was headed back home. As part of the normal "takeover" procedures, we would do "left seat, right seat" patrols. For about a week, our platoons would interchange in their roster during clearance missions, learning the routes and absorbing information from those with the experience. But they did things very, very differently.

If they saw a bit of trash that looked suspicious, they would just run it over with the mine-roller attached to the front of the vehicle. This was absolutely buck-wild to me! Our standard operating procedure would have us stop, call forward the vehicles with special tools to investigate the trash safely, clear it as not a threat, and then move on.

Can you imagine my nervous system during that first "left seat, right seat" patrol? Every single time they swerved for a piece of trash my body was screaming: "Bad idea! Bad idea!". I was operating entirely on autopilot, my survival instincts taking over.

What if I had the tool of mindfulness to help ease my awareness and be absolutely present in my body instead of controlled by expectations and programming?

While we found, and neutralized safely, about half of the IEDs we encountered (with the other half finding us, with no or few injuries resulting), this unit safely found *none* of the IEDs they encountered - they were struck by all of them. I will let you determine whose approach was more effective.

While I'm thankful for the expert guidance from my leadership that kept me safe, I often wonder if my experience in Iraq, with my specific job, might have been different had I been equipped with the tool of mindfulness.

Practice

According to Dr. Jha's research, it shows that as little as twelve minutes of mindfulness daily can produce physical differences in your brain.

- Lay down on the floor, close your eyes, put some easy music on, and just try to focus on your breath at the tip of your nose as you inhale and exhale.
- Like every other "practice," it requires patience to recognize new patterns and to build stamina. You might not make it to 12 minutes, but at least three minutes of mindfulness is better than nothing.

Pay Attention

Most "traditional" sales advice teaches you to ignore your sensations and feelings in favor of scripted responses and automatic reactions. You have to unlearn the practice of ignoring your body and rather actively observe it.

- Add a "sensations felt" section to your inventory templates or post-call review process. When the client asked a tough question, did you feel your chest tighten? When someone gives negative feedback, do your cheeks flush? Once you begin to note these feelings, you can start working with them as signals to improve your skills instead of silencing them as distractions.

Get Feedback

* Using an AI-based call analysis tool like *Sybill* can help you analyze the emotional components of your communication when you might not notice them.
* During your weekly call recording review (you're doing those, right?), ask your manager or call grader to observe any non-verbal communication you display that might clue you into the different sensations you experienced during the review.

Mindfulness is a human skill that will benefit your entire life with proper practice, but hopefully, showing how it can be implemented in sales will help you get started in your practice.

The "Hard Shit" List

One of the best ways to create an intention - that is, a description of how you aim to orient yourself towards the world - is to reflect on the types of attributes and actions you've displayed in the past. I call this my "Hard Shit" list. In other words, it is a physical repository of all the hard things I've done throughout my life.

We can't control the future, but we can gain perspective from our past experiences to prepare ourselves for the future. Perhaps you've done hard things in the past, so you may definitely do more hard things in the future.

Creating your "Hard Shit" list:
1. Set your timer to 15 minutes.
2. Write down specific examples of hard situations you've experienced in life and work.
3. Write the qualities (adjective) you displayed and the action that expressed them.
4. Display this list at a strategic point, where you will see it often to remind yourself of all the obstacles you've overcome.

Personally, I separate my "Hard Shit" list into the categories of life and work, with each category being written on a different color sticky note. I then display them on my office wall, where I can see and reflect on them.

One of my professional examples:
"Bravery - to report XXXXX to IG, to protect my soldiers in the field, to push myself in the craft of sales, and to give candid feedback at work."

One of my personal examples:
"Self-improvement - Committed to time in therapy over the years to work through my issues to be better to myself and my partner. Hard work."

Regardless of the attributes/actions, if you take the time to write out as many as you can in a fifteen to twenty-minute session, I promise you'll realize you're more of a badass than you ever give yourself credit for. You've done hard stuff in the past, and you can do hard things again in the future. You can trust yourself. By reflecting on the qualities that helped you to accomplish those hard things and overcome obstacles, you can use them clearly in your intention statement.

Putting It into Practice

Now that we've examined the science behind intention statements, the reason for their use, and their importance, it's time for you to apply the tips we've mentioned earlier. The good news is that it is impossible to get it wrong! Intention statements are entirely personal, so no one else can judge their accuracy. They're also not a "yes/no" function of correctness but rather a gradient of effectiveness.

What you need to get started:
- **Grab a pen and paper:** While typing is an option, I've discovered that the physical engagement of writing helps me internalize the statement more, and making it a part of you makes it more effective.
- **Focus on the big picture:** Your intention should reflect your life purpose, not just your career goals. Your intention should transcend just "making money."

Exercise:
1. Write Down Your Intention
Put your intention in a simple and clear sentence. It's not just about numbers. It's about your bigger purpose in life, of which

your career is just a fragment of your life purpose. This intention should speak to you and what you want to achieve in life.

Prompt: "How would I like to be in the world?"

2. **Intention Reset**
   a) Before you go into a meeting—internal or external—create space to allow yourself thirty to sixty seconds to take a couple of deep breaths and set your intention for the meeting.
   b) Clearly visualize the expected outcome, focusing on how you want the other person to feel after the meeting.
   c) Connect these mini-resets back to your overarching daily intention and think about how they align with your broader goals.

3. **Share Your Intention**
   a) Sharing your core philosophy with others can be a great tool for building trust. Intentions are captured reflections of our core philosophy - the fundamental truths that resonate with your entire being.
   b) Sometimes, our intention feels so personal that it's hard to share. Use your best judgment here, as if it feels that personal. How others react to you sharing it could introduce doubt or emotional contagion internally.

When you focus on your intention in sales, it changes your perception of success and how you handle challenges. It brings joy to your work.

My intentions shared above are just one format or example of an expression that requires introspection and creativity. Truly, they are yours to own. Your intention statement might be extremely simple or robust, but the point is to:

- **Write it down:** Physicalize your intention.
- **Believe in it:** Focus and conviction in your "why."
- **Repeat it:** Internalize them through repetition.

Remember, having an intention means always knowing the reason for your action and making sure every action is a step towards accomplishing your following goals.

CHAPTER 4:

GOALS

"When will you demand the best for yourself?"
- Epictetus

You might be wondering why we need a section to examine goals and how to set them, right? While it might seem elementary, where have your current goal-setting techniques landed you? Do you feel the need to change? If not, keep setting goals with your current technique—pick and choose what is helpful. However, if you're like the average salesperson, you might be wondering if there's a better way.

We discussed intention in the preceding chapter, which is like the compass or GPS that ensures you arrive at the correct destination. Goals, on the other hand, are similar to checkpoints or pitstops you have to make along the way to your destination. If you've ever been on a road trip, which I'm sure you have, then you know that making pitstops is a vital part of the journey. You have to stop, refresh yourself, replenish your resources, and evaluate the rest of the journey. In sales, you have to constantly pause and reevaluate yourself, your strategies, and your tactics.

Do I Need to Change?

Let's use a litmus test to examine whether this book might apply to you as a salesperson with at least a bit of experience to analyze:

1. **How many "repeat" clients have you had over the years?**
   - This could be within the same offering, at new roles/offerings, or even when they move companies and want to use your services. If you can count them on one hand, you should consider changing your ways.

2. **Outside of winning or losing—outcomes we rarely control—how does it "feel" to do your job?**
   - If you don't feel good doing your work, you either won't be able to do it long enough or will have long-term health and emotional consequences.

3. **If you were fired tomorrow, would your "best clients" hire you?**
   - Invariably, do they allow you to go so deep that you can fit in with their culture and language, build rapport with leadership, understand their business challenges, understand industry evolution, and know their clients? Are you regularly offered sales roles with your clients during your daily work? People want to solve problems with individuals they like and respect. Do you fit into this category?

4. **How often do you receive unprompted referrals from prospects or clients?**

- The results and the outcomes of our work can reveal whether our goals were effective. It allows us to assume we will achieve our goals, assume we have achieved our goals in the past, and then work backward from what that achievement looks like. If you've never explicitly defined goals that align with other parts of your work or life, don't expect the outcomes to align either.

Goals, Defined.

Steven Kotler, in *The Art of Impossible*, delivers a succinct definition of the types of objectives that are life-altering: high and hard goals. Goals are high when they're elevated and aligned with your best interest. They're hard when they're challenging to achieve.[15]

In his analysis, unlocking the "flow state" is the key to productivity. Kotler dives into pioneering psychologist Mihaly Csikszentmihalyi, whose work suggests flow often requires a "skills/challenge gap," where the challenge is 4% to 5% harder than your skills can perform.[16] Although this number seems very specific, the point is that the brain needs to feel like it is stretching itself to release the neurochemical cocktail we call the flow state.

---

15 Kotler, S. (2021). *The Art of Impossible: A Peak Performance Primer.* Harper Wave. pp. 67-68.

16 Kotler, S. (2014). *The Rise of Superman: Decoding the Science of Ultimate Human Performance.* New Harvest. pp. 57-60.

The Science Behind Goals

One of the greatest lessons I learned on this journey of creating the IGST framework is that setting goals is a fundamental human behavior instilled in us for good reason. Mounting scientific evidence shows that goals motivate us and play a crucial role in boosting our performance and overall well-being. But why are goals so effective in motivating us and driving success? Science offers some very compelling answers to this question.

A key player in the goal-setting process is a region of the brain called the *ventral striatum*. This region is associated with motivation and reward. When we set a goal and begin to work toward it, the striatum releases dopamine, which is a neurotransmitter that creates feelings of pleasure and anticipation.[17] In other words, the goal becomes the motivation, and the release of dopamine becomes the reward. This positive reinforcement loop motivates us to persist in our efforts, driving us closer to achieving our objective.

Researchers also discovered the goal-setting theory which is based on the premise that "Conscious goals affect action".[18] In other words, specific goals, as opposed to vague aspirations, create a clear roadmap for action. They allow us to track progress, identify obstacles, and adjust our strategies as needed. The keyword you need to remember when setting goals is "Specificity."

---

17   Kim, H. (2013). *Dopamine: From Motivation to Action*. Frontiers in Psychology, 4, 1-7.

18   Locke, E. A., & Latham, G. P. (2002). Building a practically useful theory of goal setting and task motivation: A 35-year odyssey. *American Psychologist, 57*(9), 705-717.

If you want a specific outcome, you need to create specific goals. Or, in the words of our marksmanship lesson from the preface: "aim small, miss small."

While setting easily achievable goals can provide a quick do-pamine boost, it's the pursuit of challenging goals that unlocks your full potential. Studies have shown that goals perceived as moderately difficult lead to greater motivation and higher levels of performance compared to easy or very difficult goals.[19] This "sweet spot" between comfort and challenge is what activates the brain's learning and growth centers, prompting us to develop new skills and stretch our abilities.

In my personal experience, setting goals transcends just achieving my objectives. The sense of purpose and accomplishment I feel from setting those seemingly impossible goals and then achieving them is unrivaled. This feat not only unlocked potentials that had laid dormant, but it also enhanced my self-esteem. I was mentally happier and healthier than I had ever been, and as a result, I had even more motivation and the ability to sustain high performance.

Tools for Setting Goals

Environment

In *The Extended Mind*, Annie Paul established that our environment becomes an extension of our mind. We do this every day

---

19 Bostan, C. M., Apostol, L., Andronic, O., Stanciu, A. V., & Constantin, T. (2022). The impact of goal difficulty on motivation and performance: A meta-analytic review. *Journal of Applied Psychology, 107*(3), 382-395.

through the things we interact with—a phone with a messaging app that we use to communicate with friends, a notebook with a to-do list, and the sticky note on our monitor so we don't forget a task. In her research, she discovered that those who intentionally use their environment as extensions of their minds become more productive in action and in achieving their goals.[20]

Just like we use external tools (smartphones, notebooks) to extend our cognitive abilities, we can leverage our physical environment to boost goal achievement. Remember the "Hard Shit" list from a previous chapter? Making it into a physical object (poster board, whiteboard) and placing it in a prominent location is an application of this principle.

Where and how we direct our gaze impacts our mood. I'm aware it probably feels like there are so many variables that affect our mood; how will you ever learn them all? Fortunately, that's not the point. The point is to learn these various factors and then stack them into consistent, repeatable habits—see *Atomic Habits* for more tips on habit stacking. By strategically placing inspirational quotes, goal reminders, or progress charts, we can create a visual landscape that reinforces our commitment to our goals. In other words, managing your environment creates a consistency in your routine that's difficult to achieve otherwise.

I encourage you to create this physical representation of your "High, hard goals", outlined by Steven Kotler in the previous chapter. Whether it is in the form of sticky notes all over your

20   Paul, A. M. (2021). *The Extended Mind: The Power of Thinking Outside the Brain*. Houghton Mifflin Harcourt. pp. 92-95.

workspace, a whiteboard with your goals written in different colors, or even a vision board. You can pick a method that resonates with you. What's important is the application of the principle.

For setting and achieving high, hard goals, it's invaluable to reflect on the hard things we've accomplished in the past. If you need a moment of clarity, just look over the board and then stare out a window and reflect—it works wonders.

Putting It into Practice:

1. Place your "hard shit" list in a location you can physically see it. Take time throughout your day to reflect on these items so they can inform your high, hard goals over time.
2. Incorporate Visual Cues. Use visual aids like vision boards, progress charts, or motivational images. These visual cues can help keep your goals at the forefront of your mind and inspire action.
3. Utilize apps and tools designed for goal setting and tracking. Apps like Trello, ClickUp, Monday.com, etc.

CHAPTER 5:

STRATEGIES

> *"Strategy without tactics is the slowest route to victory.*
> *Tactics without strategy is the noise before the defeat."*
> **- Sun Tzu**

Now that you have your "high, hard goals" set, it's time to create a roadmap with clear milestones on how to get you there. The route (strategy) you take is incredibly important because it will determine the tactics you need to apply to arrive at your destination. Whether you apply the "scenic route" or the "fastest route", they are both examples of strategies you can use to determine the specific tactics—the turns and roads in this analogy—to take on the way to your goals.

In my opinion, *The Art of War* by Sun Tzu is required reading for everyone, although it is a military treatise that discusses various aspects of warfare. You may not realize it, but you are constantly at war. Whether it is a war within your mind, a war striving to meet sales targets, or a war trying to be a great salesman, you name it. So, you cannot approach life without a plan of action. While *The Art of War* primarily focuses on military strategy, it also examines the difference between strategy and tactics. First, we will discuss strategy.

In the context of warfare, strategy refers to your overall plan or approach designed to achieve a specific objective. It involves analyzing your environment, understanding your strengths and weaknesses, and devising a long-term plan to win. This means you need to employ strategic thinking. You need to know when to sit back and observe your "enemy" and when to actively engage in battle.

When individuals preview my operating system, one of the questions often asked is the difference between strategies and tactics. The answer is simple: Strategies exist to direct tactics. You will never hear a general discussion of tactics before strategy because, without strategies, tactics can be rendered useless. For example, think of a movie or a theater production. Strategy acts as the **director**, crafting the overall vision and plan of action. It defines the "why" and "how" behind your efforts. Tactics, on the other hand, are the **actors** on stage executing the specific actions outlined by the strategy. They represent the "what" – the concrete steps taken to achieve your goals.

In other words, the journey towards achieving your goals involves a delicate interplay between strategy and tactics. Understanding the difference between these two is essential for effective action.

We rarely rely on a single strategy on our journey to success. Typically, achieving our goals involves a combination of many strategies. This approach aligns with having multiple high, hard goals across different areas of life. Each goal often requires a distinct strategy tailored to its unique demands.

For example, if you have three high, hard goals—one for finance, health, and relationship individually—you'll need different strategies for each goal.

With my current intention statement, my high, hard goals look like this:

1. **Health and Wellness**: Join the 1,000lb club in 2024. My strategy is heavy weight lifting (guided by a trainer), focusing on strength rather than hypertrophy.
2. **My Most Important Relationship**: Cultivate a deeper connection with my wife. My strategy here is to establish and maintain emotional intimacy.
3. **My Professional Life**: Become the most effective salesperson in my network. For this goal, I focus on my personalized sales methodology and this operating system.

These strategies dictate the specific tactics I employ in these three different areas of my life. There are infinite tactics to choose from, and selecting the most effective ones is beyond picking the best tactics in general, but rather those aligned with your goals and intentions. Strategies serve as the conduit for proper tactic selection.

Achieving complex goals often requires a **combination of strategies**. These strategies can complement and reinforce each other, creating a powerful synergy. For example, a business aiming to increase market share might employ a combination of strategies like product innovation, aggressive marketing campaigns, and strategic partnerships.

Strategy is typically the dimension where I often troubleshoot efforts. While you can change specific tactics, the level of strategy is normally where larger changes occur since they guide multiple tactics.

Ultimately, strategy is the practical application of your guided intention. A clear intention provides the rules to be bound by, the methods to use, and the systems to employ. I consider all these elements at the level of strategy.

In this chapter, we'll explore six (6) tried and tested strategies I have personally employed in my sales career. While these are primarily geared towards sales, you will discover that the principles transcend career lines and can also be applied to different facets of your life.

The Science Behind Strategy

The brain processes information through two primary channels: visual and verbal. Strategic thinking often involves a powerful synergy between the visual cortex and the language processing areas in the brain, which is known as "dual coding".[21]

---

21   Thomas, M. (2020). *Dual Coding and the Power of Visual and Verbal Processing in Strategic Thinking*. *Journal of Cognitive Neuroscience*, *32*(8), 1456-1463.

When we envision different strategic options, the visual cortex is activated. This allows us to literally "see" potential outcomes and simulate scenarios in our mental eye. For example, imagine it's your first day in door-to-door sales, like my story in Chapter One, and you're standing at the door of the first house. You might visualize yourself delivering a persuasive sales speech to your potential client, anticipating the client's body language, and mentally rehearsing how you'll respond to different questions and potential objections. This visual simulation, coupled with verbal processing—which helps us articulate our strategies, evaluate their feasibility, and communicate them effectively—is the essence of dual coding when it comes to strategy.

By engaging both the visual cortex and language processing areas, we create a richer and more nuanced understanding of our strategic options and potential consequences, ultimately leading to more effective strategies.

We will comprehensively examine sales strategies as we progress, but first, let's discuss strategies that can be used across diverse crafts.

Strategy #1: Deep Work

One favorite part of my craft (sales) is deep work. Don't get me wrong, there's value in activity. But sales is about effectiveness, not efficiency. It doesn't matter how efficient or active you are if you lose. And that's true for almost all knowledge work; it's almost always the quality of the work under judgment first, then the volume of the work second. If the work is full of errors, it won't matter how much gets produced.

When I first read Cal Newport's book "Deep Work," it completely altered my mindset. I realized I could stack up the hard stuff
that needs to be done—which feels good to get done—and tackle
it intentionally rather than as it comes.

"Deep Work," argues that true effectiveness hinges on the ability
to focus on cognitively demanding tasks without distraction.[22]
This is particularly true for knowledge workers, like sales, where
the quality of work – insightful conversations, strategic planning,
and compelling proposals – matters more than unproductive activities. In other words, it's not about working longer hours but
working smarter in the time you've blocked out.

Let's translate this theory into practice. Personally, here's an example of what a morning "deep work" block looks like:

1.   **Limit distractions.**
   •   I go into my office, close the door, and put on headphones.
       Some individuals recommend not checking emails or
       Slack when starting their workdays, but I have modified
       this a bit. I check and triage for only the most urgent
       items and make sure they're marked for action (stars in
       Gmail or reminders in Slack). I can settle into work better
       when I know there are no active fires—anxious brain!

22 Newport, C. (2016). *Deep Work: Rules for Focused Success in a Distracted
    World*. Grand Central Publishing. p. 3.

2. Daily journal.

- Every day, I write my intention statement, my top three goals, and my key action items for the day. Never write more than three action items that must be executed.

3. Mindfulness.

- At this point, with no distractions and my mind focused on the day, I take time to just lay still and focus on my breath. Deep breathing and meditation have the ability to elevate your day and instill the mental clarity that enables progress, which is much more effective than functioning with an anxious mind.

4. Execute.

- At this point, I work on items that require complex thinking (high-value tasks), and I don't focus on administrative or low-level tasks. This can be analyzing client data, competitor analysis, researching industry trends, developing customized sales strategies, and so on.

Here's a detailed breakdown of how I execute:

- **Call prep is always number one.** Whatever calls I have for that day or the next day, I prep out by researching the attendees, building my notes template, and sending a quick note with goals for the call. This ensures I can be on back to back calls and still be ready, even though that's less than ideal.

- **Dry runs.** Once I have prepped the call, I will practice asking the key questions I have for that specific call. I try to show up with at least a couple of practice rounds under my belt to ascertain my readiness.
- **Account planning and research.** This includes ingesting investor calls, filings, career pages, etc.
- **Briefing internal resources.** Using my read-in brief template previously shared, I'll catch anyone else who might be joining the call from my team up to speed.
- **Batching work for outbound.** Building lists, prepping call tasks with clear scripts, building messaging, but focusing on one task at a time.

I've discovered that doing deep work in my craft (sales) feels good. This doesn't mean it's easy; quite the opposite. It is often the hardest, most critical part of my day. But the feeling of knocking out tasks with the awareness that I'm making meaningful progress towards my high, hard goals is satisfying. Carrying out deep work so I can show up at my best makes me feel proud, respectful of others' time, and ready to tackle any challenge. That's why I embrace it as a broader strategy for knowledge work.

To recap: Deep work is grounded in the understanding that our brains perform best when focused intensely on a single task without distractions. To summarize deep work, we can say that it hinges on three key principles:

1.   **Attention Residue**
      - When we switch from one task to another, our attention doesn't immediately switch. Part of our mind remains

stuck thinking about the previous task, therefore reducing our cognitive capacity for the new task. Deep work minimizes this by keeping our focus on one task for extended periods.

2. **Cognitive Load**
   - Our brains have a limited capacity for processing information. Multitasking and constant distractions increase our cognitive load, leading to mental fatigue and lower-quality work. Deep work reduces cognitive load by focusing on one task at a time.

3. **Neuroplasticity**
   - Do you remember this term? Engaging in deep work strengthens the neural pathways associated with focused attention, making it easier to enter a state of flow and improve productivity over time.

Strategy #2: Extreme Ownership

If you only had the time or resources to read one book to be successful in life, I would recommend *Extreme Ownership* by Jocko Willink (*Deep Work* would be a very close second). *Extreme Ownership* is a foundational work for my career. The first time I read the book, it felt like I recognized all the best lessons I learned during my time in military leadership, summed up into a repeatable format.

Extreme Ownership presents a litmus test by which you can measure yourself and every "leader" around you during difficult situations. It reads as a business book via war memoir, encapsulating Jocko and co-author Leif Babin's time in the military, specifically Ramadi, Iraq, in 2006, into specific vignettes to support the book's framework. Wartime military leaders are put into life-or-death situations that hone the cutting edge of leadership exponentially faster than any other environment; the stakes are extremely high to tolerate poor leadership, as it can get people killed.

If diamonds are the result of millions of years of pressure and heat in the soil's crust, the lessons learned about leadership and inscribed into *Extreme Ownership* are the diamonds of war. As terrible as the experience of war is, the lessons it teaches can have a transformative impact on everyone.

My job in the Army, known as a Military Occupational Specialty (MOS), was Combat Engineer. We dealt with explosives and were often attached to other units to breach complex obstacles. Combat Engineers in the U.S. Army are the ones who lay or clear obstacles to preserve "freedom of maneuver." These roles exist across the Active component of the Army as well as in the Reserve and National Guard. We trained interchangeably across these components because we were often the spearhead of any large or sustained movement.

Imagine a pass between two mountains, and you're in a tank, tasked to pass through. One side or the other is going to have mined the pass, bracketed it for indirect fires (big booms), or set up an ambush with the kill zone in the pass.

In more recent times, Combat Engineers specialized in "route clearance": basically, finding and dealing with IEDs so routes can be safe to maneuver, ideally finding the IED before it found you. But as the Global War on Terrorism wound down in Iraq and Afghanistan, the Army pivoted towards re-building capabilities against "near-peer adversaries"—more conventional forces. Preparing to breach or build obstacles alongside infantry, armor, and cavalry in a combined effort became our unit's focus.

Now, imagine the difference in training. On one hand, you have Active Duty, full-time professional soldiers who do this type of work—regular shooting and demolition range visits, maintaining vehicles, and administrative tasks—day in and day out. On the other hand, you have us, part-time Reservists, still Professional Soldiers but with 10% of the potential training time. Both needed to meet the same standards and work interchangeably.

In fact, we attended the National Training Center (NTC) on a training rotation supporting a Combat Brigade Team with mainly Active, and some Reserve and National Guard, soldiers. That meant we had to meet the same standards for qualification and ability to safely conduct live-fire operations in our vehicles. We had to be able to keep up, do our job, and ensure no one got hurt doing it.

Along with participation in this training came a host of training and certifications for these standards. Let me break this down for you:

Engineer Qualification Tables

How well could I, as a Squad Leader of eight soldiers, command my team to complete the core competencies of our job —shoot, move, and communicate? If we patrolled deep into the mountains with Scouts to coordinate obstacle reconnaissance, we needed to blend in with the team.

Similarly, they needed to believe we were capable of doing our job—clearing a mine, breaching a wire obstacle, blowing down a door with a charge—as well as standard soldierly tasks such as shooting our weapons, communicating over radios, and performing first aid. This would allow them to attach a whole squad at a time to their companies.

There were 13 squads to qualify and certify that they were ready to attend the training. For eight months prior to the event, we drilled on every single item in the table. We studied the manuals, understood the standards expected for each task, and established a "point person" for each core competency who then cross-trained to ensure we could revolve duties if needed.

But what about using vehicles and falling in with their convoys—how could we prove our capabilities to do that safely?

Gunnery Tables

If we were going to be doing live-fire exercises on dummy targets in real-time with real ammo and explosives, we would need to pass the established Gunnery Tables. These are a series of targets a vehicle and its gunnery crew must navigate and clear to qualify.

The standards were exceedingly strict; verbal commands were graded, every target had to be hit, and consistently safe operation was required. However, the issue was that the Army Reserve had not completed Gunnery Tables in decades, if ever.

So, we found the manuals and started learning. We had some higher-level resources that helped the command team set up the training, but in terms of ensuring we qualified enough Gunnery Teams to attend this training, that responsibility fell to the platoon leadership (i.e., me).

This wasn't just going up to a firing line and hitting a target with your rifle. This was a team effort to have a vehicle maintained enough to complete the course, a gunner competent enough to operate the M2 .50 Cal and take immediate action to clear any stoppage, an assistant gunner savvy enough to prep the right amount of ammunition at the right time, and a crew leader skilled enough to orchestrate the madness. The standards were meticulous—the commands had to be followed to a T, the verbal exchange had to be exact (sentence structure was dictated and memorized), and the shots had to hit the target within a number of seconds to qualify.

The most difficult part of this for leadership was that both of these tests—Engineer and Gunnery Qualification Tables—would take place simultaneously over 10 days. We couldn't be everywhere at once. Some of our platoon was training for Gunnery Tables, some for Engineer tables, so at some point, the training and preparation had to be good enough to get the job done because leadership couldn't be everywhere with everyone at once.

As I mentioned above, I chose to lead a squad for our platoon through the Engineer Tables and let other leaders handle the Gunnery qualification. When the time finally came to perform on the Engineer Qualification Tables, I was basically accountable to two people—my platoon leader and platoon sergeant—and managed two people—my team leaders.

This "everywhere all at once" pressure worked out okay for my Platoon, as when we finally went through the EQT, our Squad qualified 1st out of 13 squads assessed, just as we told our soldiers we would if we focused on the standards of each task and performed them to our utmost abilities.

We practiced what Jocko Willink in *Extreme Ownership* calls "Decentralized Command." In this case, we made one soldier responsible as the subject matter expert for each area, then had them continuously cross-train with each other until everyone moved together fluidly as one unit. If you've ever been on a highly-trained team, you know the feeling of unconsciously-synchronized action, a byproduct of hours and hours of intentional practice. However, the six Gunnery crews were struggling. After a few attempts, their vehicles were breaking down, communications were going out, and safety violations were rampant.

The Range NCOIC—the person calling the shots and running the qualification tables—threatened that if they did not immediately turn their performance around, they would be kicked off the range, and our whole company would not be able to attend the training event at NTC.

As I was taking my gear off in our tent from the success-ful completion of the Engineer Qualification tables, one of my team leaders, a corporal, ran up to me breathless. "SGT Floyd, you need to report to the range tower and see Ser-geant First Class Brown. He said if we have one more failure, we're kicked off the range and wanted to know who would step in to take charge. I told him you could do it, so he said you're to take over the Gunnery Tables."

When I reached the top of the Range Tower, Sergeant First Class Brown, who I had previously worked with, looked at me and said, "Good, let's get this locked up. You know what to do; go do it. Your guys have 36 hours—tonight and tomorrow—to re-train and make this happen. No more mistakes or safety violations, or everyone goes home."

Of course, my first thought was for my aching feet after days of patrolling and qualifying. But I lived for the feeling of delivering results in a team environment. Human collaboration at each of our individual peak capabilities produces intoxicating results.

I quickly returned to the staging area to inspect our vehicles, ammunition, and gear—it all now fell to me to ensure every-thing went off without a hitch where previously there had only been failure.

We had started out with eight working vehicles and sets of com-munication, leaving a couple of spares for parts or backup. But now, due to vehicle and radio breakdowns, we had three func-tioning vehicles. We'd already had two disastrous attempts at the

qualification tables, with this being our third and final chance.
To be frank, the circumstances were pretty bleak. I walked over
to the dejected gunnery crews informally waiting to be given
direction for the evening.

"Alright, listen up. I know I haven't worked with all of you, but
I'm here to help.

"We brought six gunnery crews here to qualify. We are going to
leave with six gunnery crews qualified. But it's going to be a long
couple of days, and you have to follow exactly what I say. We
only have one chance to get this right.

"We've been given another chance at qualifying. We have tonight
and tomorrow to reset and get it right, and a final qualification
attempt after that.

"So here's the plan: Every vehicle will have an inventory checklist.
Drivers are now responsible for the vehicle running. Assistant
gunners are responsible for the functioning of all the equipment on the inventory checklist and ammunition preparation.
Gunners are responsible for their weapons systems, optics, and
appropriate commands. Crew leaders are now responsible for ensuring comms equipment is inventoried, works, and appropriate
commands are given.

"First, everyone will clean and inventory every vehicle, pull everything out while we still have sunlight, and present it in uniform
layout order for inspection. We will inspect the equipment while
we still have sunlight and then we will eat.

"Second, once we have all equipment inspected and vehicles stocked, we will do individual training. My crew will lead separate training sessions for Gunners, A-Gunners, and Drivers, and I will work with Crew Leads. After chow, we will train until 22:00.

"Finally, we will rehearse from 22:00 until complete. Each squad will verbally walk through each step of qualification from successfully hitting the target, back to verbal commands and sighting the target, back to the objective rally point, and finally, you will rehearse back to where we are standing.

Who here has a problem with that plan?"

There was silence. Nobody raised their hands.

"Good. Watch my crew demonstrate breaking their vehicle down and preparing it for inspection, you do the same, then I'll be by in an hour."

The rest of the story is straightforward. Everyone had a role to focus on and were trained to meet the standard. Failures were met with additional systems and procedures instead of blaming, or shaming, and the crews celebrated their changes as a team. I gave a couple of early-morning, coffee-fueled inspiration speeches, the boys hyped each other up when they did well, and the time flew by. In the end, all six teams qualified.

So, as you can see, extreme ownership is a mindset that demands full accountability for everything within your realm of responsibility, regardless of the circumstances. I'm not just about taking the blame when things go wrong but also about taking proactive steps to ensure success and addressing issues head-on before they escalate into problems.

As you have now learned from my story, the training was intense, demanding, and it required us to meet the same rigorous standards as our Active Duty counterparts, despite our limited training time as Reservists. We were expected to perform at the highest level in both Engineer Qualification Tables and Gunnery Tables, with no room for error.

Now, it would have been easier to make excuses, citing all the very valid reasons why we could not perform at the standard requested because, in all fairness and as I have already mentioned, we didn't get nearly as much training as our Active Duty Counterparts. However, I understood that excuses lose opportunities.

In this case, every soldier was held accountable. All of us were responsible. We had a non-negotiable standard to meet as a unit, not as individuals, and the only way we could achieve that was to take extreme ownership. For me, personally, this was an opportunity to prove my abilities as a leader.

Taking extreme ownership means that there is no one else to blame. When things go wrong, as they inevitably do, the onus is on you as the leader to step up, take responsibility, and find a solution. In this situation, the challenges we faced could easily have been reasons for failure—limited training time, equipment breakdowns, and safety violations. But instead of pointing fingers or looking for excuses, we took control of what we could influence.

When I was called upon to take charge of the struggling Gunnery Tables, I knew the weight of responsibility that came with it. Failure wasn't just a personal loss; it would mean the entire company couldn't attend the National Training Center, a critical training opportunity. The stakes were high, and the pressure was intense, but that is exactly when the principles of extreme ownership become most vital.

I quickly assessed the situation, identified the critical issues, and formulated a plan. However, it wasn't enough just to have a plan; execution required buy-in from the entire team. Extreme ownership isn't just about the leader taking responsibility—it's about empowering everyone to take ownership of their roles. I made it clear that each crew member had a specific job to do, and success depended on each one of us executing our part to the best of our abilities.

Through clear communication, meticulous planning, and relentless practice, we turned the situation around. The process was exhausting, and there were moments of doubt, but giving up was never an option. The team came together, focused on the mission, and ultimately, we succeeded. As you already know, all six teams qualified, a feat that had initially seemed almost impossible.

Excuses are easy to make, and they often feel justified. Yet in the end, they are just that—excuses. They don't solve problems and they don't drive success. By embracing extreme ownership, you eliminate the option of excuses. You focus on what you can control, take action to improve the situation, and learn from every challenge you face.

C.S. *Lewis* said, "You'll never know what you can do until you try, and *very few* try unless they have to." Taking extreme ownership means trying even if the situation seems impossible. The only way you will ever find out is if you take the risk in the first place. High, hard goals cannot be achieved without risk. These seemingly difficult situations will always arise to stretch you, and to elevate you to the place you need to be to turn your dreams into reality. Doing the same old thing in your comfort zone will only give you the same old, unfulfilling results.

Going back to the book *Extreme Ownership*, although its context is military, the principles resonate beautifully with the world of sales. At its core, sales is about leadership. Here are tips on how you can apply these concepts to your sales career:

1. Take Full Responsibility:
Own your sales targets, outcomes, and processes. If you miss a target, analyze what went wrong and what you can do to improve. Avoid blaming external factors like market conditions or lack of resources.

2. No Excuses for Failure:
Embrace setbacks as opportunities to learn and grow. When a deal falls through, dissect the situation to understand what could have been done differently and apply those lessons to future opportunities.

3. Plan Your Sales Strategy:

Develop a clear, actionable sales plan. Break down your goals into specific, manageable tasks and communicate them to your team. Ensure everyone understands their roles and responsibilities.

4. Communicate Effectively:

Keep open lines of communication with your team and superiors. Ensure that your team understands the overarching goals and how their work contributes to achieving them. Provide regular updates to your superiors to keep them informed and aligned.

5. Prioritize Key Opportunities:

Identify your most promising leads and focus your efforts on closing those deals. Allocate your time and resources to the tasks that will have the most significant impact on your sales performance.

6. Empower Your Team:

Trust your team members to handle their responsibilities and make decisions. Provide them with the necessary support and resources, and give them the autonomy to execute their tasks. This creates a sense of ownership and accountability within the team - "decentralized command" as Jocko calls it.

To fuse the tips, ultimately, sales is about leadership: leading yourself, your prospect, and your colleagues, toward an end goal.

Strategy #3: The 80/20 Rule

The 80/20 rule, also known as the Pareto Principle, is a powerful strategic tool for determining where to focus your energy. It posits that in any set of tasks, accounts, time, or items, 20% of the inputs will be responsible for 80% of the outcome. By concentrating on a small subset of the whole, you can make significant progress.

I use the Pareto principle in sales to determine my carrying capacity of active opportunities at any given time. For instance, if I can successfully carry five opportunities at the same time at my highest performance standards, my total opportunities in my pipeline should be around twenty-five. That's because five is 20% of 25. Similarly, if my sales process were so involved that I could only carry one major opportunity at a time, I would probably have about five open at any given time — one is 20% of five.

This leaves two major questions: how to determine your carrying capacity of open opportunities at any given time and which opportunities to prioritize in your "top five" (or top one, etc.).

How to Determine Carrying Capacity in Sales

In sales, the focus is on the decision-making process—the client's ability to decide to use or not use our offering/services. Some decisions are more involved than others, depending on the complexity of the problem your offering/service addresses. Thus, it's not feasible to evenly distribute your time across every opportunity — some might be complex with a large payoff, while others might require only a small solution for a minor problem.

In subsequent chapters, we will examine how to build a sales process to the highest standard, but at this point, let's assume you have this process built. Since sales is about effectiveness, not efficiency, our goal is to execute a highly effective process and then learn how to scale it to be the most efficient with our time.

Let's assume you have a process built that can support your "dream client." What would they look like? How big would the opportunity be? How long would it take to get to a final decision? How many people would be involved? What type of people would be involved? By envisioning and designing your ideal client in this way, you can understand how many "ideal clients" you could carry simultaneously.

Establishing a baseline of carrying capacity — i.e., showing up at your absolute best through your most effective process on X number of accounts — is the first step. Eventually, you might want to expand your carrying capacity as you progress. When your best-effort sales process is first executed, it will feel daunting. That's simply because you haven't yet automated and iterated on each step — that comes with practice. But as you refine each step in the process over time, you'll eventually be able to carry more accounts at the same time, all being served with the highest standard you have to offer.

Applying the 80/20 Rule to Prioritize Opportunities

Once your carrying capacity is determined or even improved over time, the next step is to ascertain the opportunities to apply your highest standard. In a best-case scenario, you define your ideal client, and then they materialize into your pipeline over time through your efforts. However, if you're a salesperson currently, you probably already have several opportunities open that you can apply the 80/20 rule against. Here are a few dimensions of the opportunity that should be weighed:

- **Total Amount:** What's the total amount you would earn if the sale goes great and you "win" the deal?
- **Close Date:** Which opportunities have a compelling event driving urgency nearest on the calendar? (This is not the same as randomly assigning a close date so it doesn't show up on a forecast in your CRM.)
- **Champions:** In which opportunities do you have true champions — people with organizational influence who have something to gain from your offering/service and who will sell on your behalf when you're not in the room?

While there are many other dimensions you might use to categorize what makes a "dream client" or highlight existing opportunities to find the 20% of your pipeline — how clean is the opportunity, how good is the logo as a win, what kind of one-to-many/referral impact would the win bring — I tend to prioritize opportunities where I have clear champions first, then opportunities with the closest compelling events, and finally those with the largest amount. See Nate Nasralla's book *Selling With* for an exhaustive detail on how to identify and develop champions.

If you have twenty-five open opportunities, for example, select the top five and then physically write them down — on a post-it, on a whiteboard, or in your notebook — every day. Dedicate conscious effort daily to move those five forward through your highest-effort process. There's almost always more work to be done, and sometimes you'll have to change who sits in the "top 5" list, but as the old saying goes: "where focus goes, energy flows." Narrow your focus through the application of 80/20 rule analysis, and you will achieve greater results.

Putting It into Practice:

Remember, your carrying capacity is the number of opportunities you can effectively manage at peak performance level. You can leverage the 80/20 rule to determine your carrying capacity. So, let's explain this in a clear format for easy understanding.

Step 1: Define Your "Dream Client"

- **Complexity:** Consider the decision-making process involved with your ideal client. Are their needs complex, requiring a high-touch approach, or do they seek a simpler solution?
- **Deal Size:** What's the potential revenue generated by closing a deal with your ideal client?
- **Sales Cycle Length:** How long is usually required to reach a final decision with your ideal client?
- **Decision-Makers:** How many people are involved in the decision-making process, and what are their roles?

By envisioning your "dream client," you gain a clear understanding of the ideal workload you can manage while delivering exceptional service.

Step 2: Establishing Your Baseline Carrying Capacity
Knowing how many "dream clients" you can handle simultaneously sets your baseline carrying capacity. This number might increase over time as you refine your skill set and become more efficient.

Step 3: Prioritizing Opportunities
Even with a defined carrying capacity, you likely have multiple opportunities in your pipeline. Identify the "top 20%" worthy of your highest effort by total deal value, urgency, and champion strength.

Step 4: The "Top 5" Method
Once you've identified your top opportunities, physically write them down and dedicate your focus to moving them forward through your most effective sales process. Remember, "where focus goes, energy flows."

Strategy #4: Account-Based Selling
Account-Based Selling (ABS) is a strategic sales approach that aligns the efforts of sales and marketing teams to engage, convert, and grow key accounts. This approach has been refined and popularized by many leaders in the sales space, including Heiman Miller in their seminal book, "Strategic Selling."

The essence of ABS is viewing each account as an individual market. This perspective deviates from traditional sales strategies, which often treat all customers and prospects as part of a homogeneous market. ABS calls for a tailored, personalized approach that focuses on the unique needs, challenges, and opportunities of each account. It's about understanding the intricacies of the accounts and navigating the complex web of decision-makers, influencers, and gatekeepers who determine the purchasing decisions.

Heiman Miller's work is foundational to ABS, with the concepts of "Strategic Selling" providing the backbone for this approach. The duo presents a structured methodology for managing complex sales processes, which includes understanding the buyer's decision-making process, identifying key players, and aligning your selling process with the buyer's needs. Their work has influenced how sales professionals approach ABS, enabling them to build strategic relationships and effectively navigate the complexities of large deals.

Key Tenets of ABS

A key tenet of ABS, as expounded by Heiman and Miller, is the importance of understanding the customer's organizational structure and the roles of different stakeholders. In ABS, connecting with a single decision-maker is not enough. Rather, you need to build relationships with multiple stakeholders who influence the buying decision. These may include:

- **Economic Buyers:** Control the budget.
- **User Buyers:** Use the product.
- **Technical Buyers:** Evaluate the technical aspects of the product.

In addition to understanding the customer's organization, ABS requires a deep understanding of the customer's business and industry. This involves thorough research of the account to understand its business model, strategic objectives, challenges, and opportunities. It's about understanding the context of the account and using that insight to tailor your sales approach.

Coordination Between Sales and Marketing

Another critical aspect of ABS is the coordination and collaboration between sales and marketing teams. Heiman Miller highlights the importance of aligning these teams to ensure a consistent and effective approach to engaging key accounts. This involves regular communication, shared goals, and coordinated efforts, ensuring that all customer touchpoints are consistent and reinforce the same message.

Planning and Execution

A successful ABS strategy requires careful planning and execution. Heiman Miller advocates for creating a detailed account plan that outlines your strategy for engaging the account, including your value proposition, engagement tactics, and plans for overcoming potential obstacles. This plan will guide your efforts and keep you focused on your strategic objectives.

ABS is not a quick fix or a magic bullet. It's a strategic approach that requires patience, persistence, and a deep understanding of your customers. However, when executed effectively, it can yield significant results, including deeper customer relationships, larger deal sizes, and increased customer loyalty.

The Biggest Payoff: Latency

As an AE using an account-based strategy for new business, I've found that the biggest payoff is latency. High-quality work done once continues to pay off quarters after we targeted accounts. I still receive "inbound" leads from previously named account targets to date. When these accounts revert to us, they typically:

1. **Understand our broader offering:** Our messaging's goal — not action.
2. **Are a well-fit account:** As we selected them carefully.
3. **Have existing project momentum:** They come in at their timing, not our outreach.

This latency effect is a product of high-quality work. When volume compromises quality, it's lost:

1. **General messaging:** It's less relevant to individual accounts, so when the need arises, they don't remember that specific email.
2. **Tangential fit accounts:** Dropped into outreach to hit numbers.
3. **Lack of project momentum:** If our messaging was never consumed, we wouldn't exist on their radar.

The Value of High-Quality Work

While it's possible to find and win new business with a scatter-shot or "spray and pray" approach, the quality of that business can suffer. The accounts may infer a lack of customization and care from the one-size-fits-all messaging, and the long-term effectiveness of such strategies is questionable.

Instead, I spent time selecting accounts that resembled successful clients, had some awareness or use of our category, and discussed what project momentum looked like for their specific use case. While those efforts weren't immediately rewarded, the end goal wasn't immediate (inside quarter) production.

The most important reward to me, as a seller, for an account-based approach is doing high-quality work I can feel good hanging my hat on, whether it's immediately effective or not. Doing high-quality work is the safest way to bet on yourself. No playing the algorithm, gaming subject lines, or using hacks/tricks.

In my case, I proactively invested in working this way before my company ever formalized an account-based approach elsewhere. You always make a choice on how you sell, whether you choose it intentionally or not. Consistent, high-quality work is a product of the systems used to produce it. Investing in systems that produce high-quality work is the key.

For more on this approach, check out my appearance on the podcast *30 Minutes to President's Club*, episode 134.

Strategy #5: Working Cross-Functionally

The Importance of Trust
Trust is the first element of a successful team. In today's complex world of B2B sales, success often hinges on the ability to build a strong, cross-functional team. However, traditional leader-

ship styles that rely on authority may not translate well in this environment.

One of the greatest lessons from Jocko Willink's *"Extreme Ownership"* is to decentralize command: push, to the lowest level possible, the authority/ability to gather, analyze, and make decisions on data. For that consistent feedback loop of assessment to be successful, however, your team must be bound by trust. You can have access to all the data in the world, but if your team is not bound by mutual trust between the team members, they won't take the risks necessary to execute audacious goals to the highest level.

Signs Your Team is Lacking Trust

- Your teammates don't feel comfortable airing observations openly.
- Your teammates all have consistent, similar themes in obstacles without management addressing them.
- Your teammates are hamstrung, waiting for the "green light" or approval to take the correct action.

You don't need to be a manager to lead. Conversely, if you're a manager and these symptoms are present within your team, then I'm sorry to inform you that you're not leading.

Building Trust Without Formal Authority

Most salespeople involved in complex B2B selling are expected to build a cross-functional team of resources to win big opportunities. This creates a quandary for those used to leading by title without trust. So, how do you build trust in an environment where no one reports to you?

Keith Ferrazzi, in his book "*Leading Without Authority*," provides the exact recipe. While the book is helpful, its learnings can be easily summarized into two words: **Go first**. By being the first person to lead with vulnerability—offering value with no expectation of return, being open about your blockers and how your teammates can help, and sharing emotions you might be feeling around the project—you tap into our hardwired biological processes of reciprocity, trust-building, and social bonds.[23]

I've found it helpful when building a "coalition" on behalf of clients to think of the effectiveness of my coalition in terms of a bank account. In an ideal world, you'd want to make deposits into your account before making a withdrawal so that you don't overdraft. Too many deposits, and you're probably losing out on returns; this part of the metaphor is also true for us, as you can over-index on what you offer/extend to your coalition members if you don't have a way to capitalize on their help in an immediate project.

This is also true for prospects. You can't just give and never receive anything in return. One of the largest discoveries I've had in the last few years is that it's all the same work, whether working with prospects from other organizations or colleagues internally, being

---

23   Ferrazzi, K. (2020). *Leading Without Authority: How the New Power of Co-Elevation Can Break Down Silos, Transform Teams, and Reinvent Collaboration.* Currency. pp. 56-58.

able to analyze where people are against where they're going, and how best they work, involves the same skill set.

If I were considering a fresh slate for coalition building—either because I moved companies, started a new role, or moved product areas—I would make it my second priority to learn about my teammates. Just like working with your prospects, to effectively lead your colleagues, you'll need to understand:

- **How are they professionally measured and compensated?** Do they work under OKR-based goals, or are they compensated based on an incentive plan?
- **What are some of their current pains and problems?** If they have an immediate need to be more successful at their job, could one of your projects be used to help?
- **What are their goals?** Do they want to get promoted?
- **How are they motivated?** While it can help to understand the financial implications of the measurements mentioned above, some people are also motivated by shoutouts, gift-giving, or positive feedback to leadership.

While understanding compensation structures is vital, remember that motivation goes beyond money. Some people value public recognition, small gifts, or positive feedback shared with leadership. This is why it's important to lead with vulnerability so you can build trust, even without formal authority.

Strategy #6: Finding
the Right Environment

The most important strategy for enabling your success in sales is discovering the right environment. Being a long-term individual contributor in sales takes finesse to avoid pitfalls. Here are some common tips to be aware of:

1. Micromanagers

Even if you find a good company, your manager might still interfere in your business. Managing activities and not outcomes is a sign of RUN. Even if you're successful, it will be despite your manager—you don't need that extra weight.

2. Comp Plan Tricks

Windfall clauses and similar tricks are designed to keep the company from losing money, not to make it awesome to be a seller. It's almost impossible to determine unless you access the actual plan or there are detailed reviews on platforms like RepVue. Even asking the existing AEs might not work because how many of them actually read and understand the plan?

3. Hungry Teammates.

Although I deeply care about integrity - doing right by myself and others - not everyone has this approach. Just remember, sales karma is a thing, and what goes around comes around. Work the accounts that are rightfully yours, pass along the ones that aren't, and do the right thing.

4. Salespeople Reputation
Your buyers generally dislike working with salespeople, and rightfully so after pushy techniques and downright lies. Working with generations of that detritus can make it difficult when you're honestly trying to do right by clients.

5. Product Market Fit
Not every product fits the market you're placed in. You might have great PMF at your company, but it's just not in your segment or your assigned product. Pre-Series B startups or new offerings are particularly suspect here.

6. Need vs. Nice
Not every product is necessary. Selling a "nice-to-have" product is possible but requires much higher levels of execution. "Need-to-have" products can be sold messy and still win, because they are business-critical.

7. Company Delivery
Even if you do your job, your team might still suck at onboarding, or the product might not work as advertised. Despite your best efforts, you can be guilty by association.

8. Losing
In sales, you lose a lot. Some companies have goals that account for 50% of their team failing to hit quota. Leaders can still get their bonuses while half the team fails. Too high of a win rate, and you get criticism for not having enough pipeline. These setups are designed for you to experience regular losses.

How to Find the Right Environment

We've just examined the types of environments to avoid, but it's equally important to know how to find the right environment.

1. **Research Thoroughly:** Gather information about the company culture, management style, and compensation plans.

2. **Ask the Right Questions During Interviews:**
   - How does the company measure success in sales?
   - Can you describe the management style here?
   - What are the common challenges salespeople face in this company?
   - How are salespeople compensated, and what are the specific terms of the company plan?

3. **Network with Current and Former Employees:** Reach out to people who have worked at the company to get acquainted with the real working environment and any potential red flags.

4. **Assess the Product and Market Fit:**
   - Research the product's market position.
   - Understand the target segment and its challenges.
   - Evaluate whether the product is a "need-to-have" or "nice-to-have."

5. **Evaluate Company Reputation and Integrity:** Look for signs of a positive sales culture and ethical behavior. Avoid companies with a reputation for underhanded tactics or a cutthroat internal environment.

By carefully evaluating potential employers and being aware of these common pitfalls, you can find an environment that supports your success and allows you to thrive as a long-term individual contributor in sales.

Stress Management

Finally, a strategy wouldn't be complete without stress management. The modern world throws a constant barrage of demands at individuals, which causes stress. Unattended stress can act like a virus, infiltrating and disrupting even the most meticulously crafted strategy. However, by incorporating stress management into your strategy, you build a **strategic firewall**, protecting your goals and boosting your ability to navigate challenges with focused intention.

Stress, in its unmanaged state, can become a strategic Trojan Horse, silently sabotaging your efforts from within by activating the following:

- **Cognitive Impairment:** Excessive stress can impair cognitive functions such as memory, attention, and problem-solving skills. This can hinder your ability to adapt your strategies as situations evolve and even devise effective tactics for said strategies.[24]
- **Tunnel Vision:** Stress narrows your focus, making it difficult to see the bigger picture and consider alternative strategies. You become fixated on immediate problems, neglecting potentially crucial long-term considerations.

---

24 Des Marais, J. (2022). *The Impact of Stress on Cognitive Function: Implications for Strategic Thinking and Adaptability. Journal of Applied Psychology, 67*(4), 233-245.

- **Consistency in Execution** Stress can lead to inconsistency in executing strategies. When stress levels peak, sticking to a plan becomes challenging, resulting in erratic actions and reduced effectiveness.
- **Decision Fatigue:** Constant stress depletes your mental resources, leading to decision fatigue. When faced with tactical choices within your strategy, you're more likely to make suboptimal decisions or avoid them entirely.

Reframing Your Stress Mindset

The way you perceive stress significantly impacts your response. Research suggests that viewing stress as a **challenge** rather than a threat can lead to improved health, productivity, and well-being. By adopting a "stress-is-enhancing" mindset, you can leverage the surge of energy associated with stress and channel it into focused action.[25]

The constant fight-or-flight response triggered by perceiving stress as a threat can have detrimental physical consequences. Shifting your mindset reduces the stress response, leading to better overall health. Stress can be paralyzing, but a challenge mindset allows you to channel that energy into focused action. You become more productive and achieve more within a short time. Unfortunately, challenges are inevitable, and viewing stress as such allows you to develop greater resilience against it.

25   Crum, A. J., Salovey, P., & Achor, S. (2013). Rethinking stress: The role of mindsets in determining the stress response. *Journal of Personality and Social Psychology, 104*(4), 716-733.

Actionable Strategies:

- **Positive Self-Talk:** Counter negative thoughts with encouraging affirmations. Instead of saying, "I'm so stressed, I'll never meet this deadline," reframe it as, "This deadline is challenging, but I have the skills and resources to succeed."
- **Cognitive Reframing:** Reinterpret stressful situations as opportunities for learning and growth. Ask yourself, "What can I learn from this challenge? How can I use this experience to improve?".

Harnessing the Power of Stress

Stress, when viewed positively, can enhance your cognitive function and physical health. Jamieson et al. (2010) found that interpreting your body's stress response (e.g., a racing heart) as a positive response to a challenge can improve your performance. Think of it like a car engine revving up – it's providing the necessary power to handle a difficult situation.[26]

"Believe it or not, stress can increase your alertness, energy levels, and ability to focus, all of which are crucial for tackling high-stakes situations."[27]

---

26   Jamieson, J. P., Nock, M. K., & Mendes, W. B. (2010). Mind over matter: Reappraising arousal improves cardiovascular and cognitive responses to stress. *Journal of Experimental Psychology: General, 139*(3), 417-431.

27   Hamilton, J. (2022). *The Upside of Stress: Harnessing Stress for Peak Performance. Journal of Health Psychology, 27*(8), 1123-1135.

By viewing these physiological changes as a natural part of the body's preparation for action, you can leverage them to your advantage.

Actionable Strategies:

- **Mindfulness Meditation:** Meditation helps you observe your thoughts and feelings without judgment. By becoming aware of your stress triggers, you can develop a more controlled response.
- **Controlled Breathing Techniques:** Deep, slow breaths activate the relaxation response in your body, counteracting the fight-or-flight response triggered by stress.
- **Visualization:** Visualize yourself successfully navigating a stressful situation. This mental rehearsal can boost your confidence and improve your performance under pressure.

A calm and focused mind allows for clear and strategic thinking. You're better equipped to analyze situations, consider options, and make sound choices aligned with your goals. While you can never eliminate stress completely, you can develop strategies to transform negative stress into positive stress and leverage it to assist you in achieving your high, hard goals.

CHAPTER 6:

TACTICS

> *"First, say to yourself what you would be;*
> *then do what you have to do."*
> **- Epictetus**

In the realm of sales, there is an infinite array of tactics at your disposal. However, the effectiveness of these tactics hinges not on their inherent qualities but on their alignment with your broader strategy and intention. The tactics provided in this chapter serve as examples specifically tailored for salespeople, illustrating how they integrate into a larger strategic framework.

Remember, there are **infinite potential tactics** available. The key lies in selecting tactics that **align with your broader system**. For instance, in my sales methodology, "multi-threading" is a tactic that aligns with my broader problem-solving strategy of Change-Based Selling.

In B2B sales, multithreading refers to the strategic practice of engaging with multiple decision-makers within a potential client organization **simultaneously**. This doesn't mean giving each person your undivided attention at the same time but rather cultivating relationships and progressing conversations with various stakeholders throughout the sales process. In any organization, decision-making is rarely confined to a single individual. By relying on only one contact, you risk losing the deal if that person leaves the company, changes roles, or simply loses interest.

Multi-threading aligns with my change-based selling strategy because it allows me to address multiple aspects of a client's challenge simultaneously, allowing me to achieve higher close rates. Knowing all of this is great, but *why* do we do it? Multithreading is a great tactic because B2B sales is about solving problems through change. Every business has multiple problems to solve and limited resources, so a problem that is worth solving is one that affects multiple people (e.g., finance, marketing, legal) as opposed to just one individual.

This example demonstrates the connection between one of my tactics and my broader sales strategy. In other words, your focus should be on **strategic alignment**, not fixed on specific tactics. That is the key. You need to identify tactics that resonate with your overarching goals and strategic framework, not only tactics that have a proven win rate.

I often feel empathy for new salespeople. They might start their careers with gusto, leaning into self-improvement and trying every little tip under the sun to get better. It's easy to feel overwhelmed when there are different tasks to accomplish, a different book to read, or another tactic to employ.

However, if you've made it this far, you should understand that the tactics that work best are those that have a broader strategy to govern their use in support of high, hard goals. With the focal point for your energy narrowed, it becomes easier to not only execute the tactics but also select which tactics suit you.

The purpose of this book is not necessarily to teach you specific tactics because I'm also not teaching you specific strategies. Instead, below is a list of tactics you can deploy to improve your role. It is important to remember that there is a myriad of tactics out there that you can align to your specific strategies. These are just examples to help you get on the right track.

Tactic #1: Heuristics

A heuristic is a helpful self-discovery device for immediate/short-term analysis. They're incredibly valuable in sales and can be used frequently, whether consciously or not. Here are two examples of heuristics:

1. **Hanlon's Razor:** "Never attribute to malice that which can be explained by stupidity, laziness, or incompetence."
   - **Example:** Your competitor sends collateral to your prospective client that has outdated information about your offering. Sure, you could say this was intentional lying. Or maybe they have humans managing their collateral, and humans aren't omnipotent and are sometimes lazy.

2. **Occam's Razor:** "The simplest explanation is the most likely."
   - **Example:** You're following up with your client multiple times, and you construct a story that they hate you and don't want to talk to you anymore. Or, it could be that they're just busy—which is simpler?

Tactic #2: Problem Statements

Problem statements are effective tools because everyone loves to talk about their problems. It's part of human nature! Not only will they talk about their problems, but if you summarize their problem for them, they'll love to remind you of the details you might have missed.

In sales, we often speak with individuals who describe their pain. Unfortunately, pain is not the same as a problem.
   - **Example:** If you're in finance and it takes a week at the end of every month to pay your contractors, the pain might be the time required and chasing down errors. But the problem is that you're processing manually instead of using an automated platform.

When my clients have a pain point, they're telling me how/where it hurts, not why.

As a salesperson, it's my job to help identify pain and translate it into a problem statement collaboratively with my buyer. Why does the pain matter to the business, and what is the problem causing the pain? At the end of the conversation, they'll at least walk away with clarity about their problem, which in itself is valuable.

You're robbing them of that clarity and help if you immediately skip to your solution rather than hear them speak about pain.

Nate Nasralla, in *Selling With*, presents the absolute gold standard for using problem statements during the sales process.

Tactic #3: Business Case

The first two tactics involve understanding and identifying problems, so the next logical step is to build a business case. A business case justifies the investment your solution offers to the client's business by outlining the benefits and return on investment (ROI).

It's important to note that your intention, and your strategy, makes a huge difference in the outcome of your business case. As Jeffrey Lipsius says in *Selling to the Point*: *"The point of selling isn't selling; the point of selling is buying."*[28] And people buy for their own reasons.

As you build your business case, the justification for why the business so enact this change at this time, in the midst of an infinite number of possible problems to solve, it's crucial to remember that the business case is about their reasons. It's not a slide deck plastered with your logos and product details.

---

28   Lipsius, J. (2016). *Selling to the Point: Because the Information Age Demands a New Way to Sell*. Xlibris. p. 12.

It's a tool that your champion will be asked to use to justify their advocacy for the question: "Why should we change right now with that specific vendor?"

The quicker you get to their language, and their reasons for buying, the better your chances of success.

The easiest way to think of a business case is as a formalized story. Like any other story, it needs clear parts:

- **Executive Summary:** What's the two to three sentence summary of the situation and recommended solution.
- **Context/Background/Summary:** How did we get here? What
- **Problem:** Typically in the form of a problem statement, highlighting the quantified impact of the problem on the business, the scope of the business being impacted by the problem, the cost of inaction in the face of the problem, and the solutions that haven't worked.
- **Solution:** While this is the section where you could highlight your offering, your offering is typically not the only part of the solution. It might be part of a broader roll out, program, or change in the business.
- **Payoff:** What good things happen as a result of implementing the recommendation of the business case?
- **Investment:** How much will it take to solve the problem presented? This should include not only the cost of your solution, but also the opportunity costs of picking this solution, the broader costs associated with a solu-

tion like yours, and the internal resources needed to make it happen.

- **Plan:** Finally, wrap up with all the details as fleshed out as possible, including the risks typically associated with a plan like this and how you will mitigate them.

Ultimately, sales is about change; big change = big sale, small change = small sale, no change = no sale. While a business case isn't a sure-fire win in sales, it's a *necessary* tool to frame up any major change.

There are entire books written about building business cases, so I won't go much further here. For more information, I'd highly recommend *Selling With* by Nate Nasralla.

Tactic #4: Daily Planner

"Parking Lot"

The parking lot is a particularly valuable tactic in sales, where pre-call jitters or worries about objections can hinder effective communication. But how does this work? Imagine you're preparing for an important call with a potential client. During your planning, a distressing concern about an upcoming deadline pop into your head. You might get sidetracked, scrambling to address the deadline, or letting the anxiety cloud your call preparation. With the parking lot tactic, you acknowledge the concern, but instead of dwelling on it, mentally "park" it in this metaphorical parking lot. This frees up your mind to fully engage in call planning.

The next day, I'll then do my journaling and add any items from the "parking lot" section of my previous day's journal onto my current day's action items. This continuity ensures the ball isn't dropped on any key items and also gives you a good pulse check on how frequently you're closing out your major items.

Pre-Call Rituals

I avoid getting "pumped up" before important calls. From my experience, being in a heightened state contradicts curiosity, empathy, and conciseness, which are crucial in sales and every other aspect of life.

Instead, over the past two years, I've developed a preparation routine for calls. Before each call, I take a moment to consider the people involved and how I want each of them to feel by the end of our conversation. I've even included the feeling statement in my executive briefs when I bring in leadership or other resources to my calls. "We want to leave them feeling…" This might go against the grain, but it's backed by solid science.

In "Psyched Up," Daniel McGinn studied various high performers—musicians, athletes, military personnel, and entertainers—to understand exactly what they did before successful performances.[29] One might imagine last-minute cramming of plans, reviewing musical notations one final time, or rehearsing lines until taking the stage. However, McClain found that the best performers don't rely on such tactics. Unlike the intense preparation that is more common in high school athletics,

29 McGinn, D. (2017). *Psyched Up: How the Science of Mental Preparation Can Help You Succeed.* Portfolio.

where teams make it to State and push even harder to win big games, successful performers prioritize consistency, routine, and ritual as essential to their success—it's a way of life, not just a fleeting boost.

The next time you plan your day or week ahead, especially before "big" moments like client calls or any other instance where the outcome is important, resist the urge to rush or inflate the importance of each interaction. You don't run around like a headless chicken and overextend yourself, knocking down meaningless tasks in an attempt to ease your anxiety. Should you mentally build up the call as if it's career-defining? Definitely not. Rather, take two to five minutes to pause, reflect on the emotions you aim to cultivate within yourself and others, remove any excess energy (read *Psyched Up* for more details on this), and just enjoy the moment.

Tactic #5: Taking Ownership - Build Your Process

In the dynamic world of sales, there's a fundamental truth that resonates across every interaction, every pitch, and every deal—every salesperson has a unique style. This individuality is a powerful asset. It's what helps you forge genuine connections with clients, stand out from the crowd, and, ultimately, close deals. But how can you harness this individuality and channel it into a structured, effective sales process that can be repeated and refined over time? The answer lies in autonomy.

Embracing autonomy means taking ownership of your sales process. It's about defining a method that aligns with your strengths, your understanding of the product, and the unique needs of your clients. Autonomy in sales is not about working in isolation or disregarding proven strategies. Instead, it's about crafting a process that synchronizes with your identity as a salesperson.

Start by identifying your strengths and areas for improvement. Are you natural at building rapport but struggle with technical details? Or do you excel in product knowledge but find it challenging to engage clients emotionally? Understanding your skills and growth areas provides a foundation upon which you can build your process.

Once you've identified your strengths and areas for improvement, it's time to create your sales process. While you should certainly leverage proven sales methodologies and strategies, remember to personalize them. Adapt them to your style, your product, and your clients. This might involve changing the sequence of steps, using different communication channels, or even incorporating unique elements like storytelling or humor.

By crafting the sales process, I mean literally writing it down step by step. Will there be some fringe cases that don't use each step - sure. However, writing out the entire process, as you want to run it, gives you an entirely new view of the sales cycle. It's no longer stages in a CRM, but a living, collaborative engagement.

Remember, the goal is not to craft a perfect sales process immediately but to create a starting point that you can refine over time.

This is where autonomy truly comes into play. As you gain more experience, you'll learn what works and what doesn't, what resonates with your clients, and what falls flat. Use this knowledge to continuously refine your sales process, making it more effective with every iteration.

Embracing autonomy also means taking responsibility for your learning and growth. Seek feedback, both from your clients and your peers. Invest time in self-reflection, examining your successes and failures to glean insights. And above all, commit to ongoing learning. Whether it's improving your product knowledge, enhancing your communication skills, or understanding your clients' industries better, there's always something you can learn to become a better salesperson.

Finally, remember that autonomy does not mean disregarding the support and resources available to you. Leverage the knowledge of your peers, the insights from your managers, and the tools provided by your organization. Autonomy is about using these resources to complement your personal style and enhance your sales process.

Tactic #6: Call Your Account-Level Plays

Determining how you'll approach your accounts is a crucial step to leverage your investments in deep work, coalition building, and all the other tactics we've discussed. Once you've identified which accounts to prospect, the next step is to decide the best way to initiate contact. However, not all approaches to account entry are equally effective.

One of the fascinating aspects of sales is the variety of approaches available. For instance, targeting Coca-Cola could involve cold calling, a colleague introduction, or leveraging a board member for credibility.

However, not all methods are equally efficient (cold calling requires more effort than an executive introduction) or effective (some methods yield higher win rates). Here's how to identify the most efficient and effective routes for you:

- Understand your metrics and data insights. (e.g., conversion rates at different stages of the sales funnel, average deal size, lead generation sources)
- Map out the account landscape and potential opportunities. (e.g., reviewing annual reports, competitor analysis, and social listening to understand company culture)
- Outline your strategic plays. (For example, for a company that values efficiency, a data-driven cold email with a clear value proposition might be most effective. For a company that prioritizes relationships, a warm introduction might be a better first step)

With this groundwork laid, it's time to implement your "plays." The unique aspect of sales is that we operate under a mandate (sales quota) but have the autonomy to achieve it through our own strategies. Here's where you can showcase the power of your personal approach and how it translates into achieving your sales goals.

Communication Tactics

During my time in basic training, one of the more intense experiences was when a fellow trainee went AWOL (Absent Without Leave). It was during a night shift on firewatch duty, which is basically a task that requires soldiers to be on guard throughout the night. Each shift would have to be covered 25%, so half of the class would be awake, and would you know, that's often when any shenanigans would go down. There was always one person in charge of each shift that the drill Sgt went to at the change of the shift to get inspected and stuff like that.

As the leader of my shift, I made my rounds to confirm that we had enough people in their bunks, matching the count of soldiers in our platoon. But after completing the check, I realized we were one person short. At some point during the night, possibly between the last shift and when I checked, a trainee had jumped out of a second-story window and went on the run.

Basic training wasn't exactly fun, but come on, you can stick it out for a couple of weeks. I immediately gathered the other privates on the shift and informed them of what had happened. Some of them suggested letting the next shift catch it during their checks. But I knew better. If we didn't report it, the drill sergeants would find out anyway, and that would make things ten times worse for everyone. I could already imagine the entire platoon being punished—gassed during PT, exhausted, and all because we didn't do the right thing.

Since I was the lead on this shift, I knew the responsibility fell on me. If we tried to let this slide, it would be my ass on the line. We were just three weeks away from graduating a 16-week course, and there was no way in hell I was going to risk having to redo it all! So, despite the anxiety that was basically strangling me, I went downstairs to report the situation to the drill sergeant on duty that night.

She wasn't from my platoon, so I wasn't familiar with her. She was the head drill sergeant for the 3rd platoon, which had a different specialty but shared our basic training. We had three platoons to the company, and one company to the barracks. So, I was unfamiliar with her. All I knew was her steely stare and cocked hat made me not want to be on the receiving end of her wrath.

I knocked on her door, stood at attention, and prepared myself for whatever was coming. As the head drill sergeant for the other platoon, she was a Bridger, the patch on her shoulder indicating she had deployed to Iraq doing such work. I swallowed hard and prepared myself, assuming the position of attention, before raising my hand and knocking on the door three times.

"What do you want, Private?" she barked in a gruff, commanding tone.

"Drill Sergeant, after completing our count, we discovered there is one private unaccounted for," I replied, trying to keep my voice steady.

"WHAT?!?!" she roared, her eyes narrowing as she processed the information.

Immediately, she went on the intercom, waking the entire company to perform an accountability formation. Then she turned her fiery gaze back to me.

"Who?" she asked coldly.

"Drill Sergeant, the missing trainee is Private Jones, Drill Sergeant," I answered.

"When did you discover this?" she demanded.

"Drill Sergeant, after performing our third round of the shift, at 03:47 AM, Drill Sergeant."

"Get outside, Private!" she ordered.

"Yes, Drill Sergeant," I replied, immediately sprinting outside to join my fellow trainees.

Following on my heels, she strode like a predator in front of the formation. With the commands, "Company, Attention!" and "Half-right Face!" we knew we were dead meat. We were "smoked"—a combination of push-ups, jumping jacks, burpees—until the company leadership arrived to take over the situation. That meant a nasty First Sergeant rolling up, who had a distinct pleasure in seeing privates suffer. We skipped our normal PT that morning, donned our uniforms, and began making a mud pit of the drill field with our low crawling. It was a long, miserable morning, with our "remediation" activities continuing until lunch.

Although we were doomed to suffer regardless, I knew I had done the right thing. By staying true to my value of integrity, I only suffered physically. If we had tried to cover it up or pass the responsibility, it would have been far worse. Integrity guided my decision, and it kept me in alignment with my intentions.

Brief Your Resources

"Never win alone, never lose alone" – a crucial lesson I've learned about sales while working at Deel. But how do you involve others, especially busy executives, in your calls? It all starts with a brief – you have to catch them up to speed.

Your goal is not to perfectly summarize every detail about the account. Your goal is to quickly (30 seconds) orient your key resources for success on the call. Send it out early, before the key date, but not so early that it becomes hard to find.

Personally, I always share the feelings I want the prospects to experience during the call.

Below is a template for my executive brief, to be used any time you bring another teammate into a call as a resource:

Section 1 – The Client
- **Business Name:**
- **Use Case/Product:**
- **Size/Scope/Stage:**

Section 2 – The People
- **People on the call:**
  - Who are the individuals on the call from the client's side?
  - LinkedIn link for quick access
  - Relevant interview/podcast/video quotes or other tidbits

- **Who's joining from your side?**

Section 3 – The Context
- **Why Change?**
  - Why does the client need to make a change?
- **Why Change with Us?**
  - Why does the client need to choose us to help with the change?
- **Why Change with Us Now?**
  - Why does the client need to do this now?

Section 4 – The Call
- **The goal of the Call:**
  - What is the purpose of the call?
  - What feelings do we want them to have at the end of the call?
- **Next Step Desired:**
  - What are the specific tasks you plan to have as the next steps?
- **Don't Do:**
  - Which topics to avoid or hot-button issues need to be handled delicately?

Pre-Call Checklists

During my days in the military, I was meticulous about checks and inspections. This obsession began before I was ever in a leadership role. During a route clearance mission, –we surprisingly came across an IED (improvised bomb). It was a routine for us, as our mission was to find and neutralize IEDs on the routes we patrolled.

After finding the IED, we sat for hours waiting for EOD (the bomb squad) to arrive so they could collect evidence and safely neutralize it. I was a gunner for my vehicle, so my primary responsibility was maintaining the weapon and ensuring our safety. Our truck was uniquely manufactured to carry the bomb squad robots you see in movies, complete with a spare battery.

When EOD finally arrived, their robot died halfway out to the IED! However, we still had our own. So, they asked to use ours to retrieve their robot and complete the task. As we deployed our robot, it died immediately. Dead battery. I was livid. It wasn't my job to ensure the batteries were charged, but this oversight put us all in danger- lack of proper tools and too much time on a target can be deadly! Luckily, we had a spare battery to use, and EOD took care of business.

I realized that important tasks - even if not directly under my control - could have huge impacts if they aren't done well. No one's perfect, so we all fail to the level of our supporting systems and processes. So, I became a stickler for checks and inspections. Both begin with a clear outline of what's expected.

In my current role, I don't sell a physical good that needs to be checked for charge. But I do have:

- Calls where I need to show up with relevant information, or we're all wasting our time (the most valuable commodity).
- Teammates who need to be briefed should join calls and catch up to speed.
- Teammates involved in our strategy who need to be in lockstep with my messaging.

So, checking that we're all aligned and even "inspecting" (i.e., dry runs, pre-calls, and reviewing details), can make or break the tough moments.

Cold Calling Quadrants

Cold calling has to be one of the hardest things in the world to do. That's coming from a guy who made it out of Iraq! Not knowing whether you're interrupting the prospect's day, if the number is even active, or if the email will just filter to spam can all have a detrimental affect on your mental stamina.

Cold calling doesn't have to be hard, or interruptive. It can actually be incredibly valuable, if you're properly prepared, researched, and know exactly *why* you're calling *that person* at *that time.*

How you feel about the cold call will determine how successful you are with it. Humans are innately capable at reading the tone of others and want to speak and spend time with those that know their stuff. Making sure you know who you're calling, what they do, and why you're calling them specifically will ensure you're as prepared as you need to be to cold call anyone.

Like in the Gunnery Tables example above, with any hard thing we start by breaking it down into its requisite parts and then iterating for improvement. Cold calls can be broken down into four key parts; the introduction, the pattern interrupt, the hypothesis, and the close. I like to visualize each of these parts in a simple two over two quadrant. I then make a quadrant for each of the key titles I'll call into, based on seniority.

For example, at Deel, I sell to HR and Finance decision makers. How we approach a CFO is drastically different then how we approach an Accounting Manager. As a result, breaking out the quadrants by seniority - ie having a quadrant built for finance leaders like CFOs or SVPs and a quadrant built for business user roles like Accounting Managers or Controllers - allows me to have full confidence that I know my stuff going into the call.

Part One - the Introduction.
The goal of the introduction isn't to fully introduce yourself, or be nice to the prospect, but to buy you additional time on the call. The first five seconds of the introduction will determine if you get the next thirty seconds of their attention. This should be fairly easy to memorize, and practice, for the best tone and delivery. There are multiple introductions to choose from - permission-based openers, "how's it going", or rapid questioning.

Personally, I like to call out the elephant in the room - you don't know me, Ms. Prospect, but I'm calling because I've done my research and worked with others like you.

Typically, the introduction also includes an ask for the additional time: "Can I share why I called?"

Part Two - Set the Table

Sparking curiosity actually comes down to a scientific formula. George Loewestein, an American Economist, postulated that curiosity could be created from an information gap. Asking a question that immediately establishes both a pattern interrupt - "whoa, this isn't a normal salesperson" - and alludes to hidden knowledge - "they know something I'd like to know" - results in curiosity and continued conversation.

Part Three - The hypothesis.

You should be rock solid on exactly why you're reaching out to this specific person and how you can help them. This can be as simple as a single sentence, or as complex as multiple points researched from their public filings. For younger companies without many case studies to rely on, this might come in the form of a hypothesis about the pains they're probably experiencing with their current state. For more mature companies, this might be comparing and contrasting their current state with the "before state" of a case study client and the results that followed.

Part Four - Close the call.

The goal of the cold call is to get in and get out as quickly as possible, so as to be as minimally disruptive as possible. While that might require an extended conversation if the prospect is open to it, some form of "I know I called you out of the blue and probably interrupted your work; are you available Thursday morning for 15 minutes to chat through this further?" typically works. Getting a specific time confirmed, with their email booked in the calendar invite, also ensures you get the result you want (a conversation with a prospect ready to chat).

Cold calling is a form of art and there have been so many books written about it. I'd specifically recommend two: *Cold Calling Sucks (and That's Why It Works)* by Armand Farrokh and Nick Cegelski[30], and *Fanatical Prospecting* by Jeb Blount.[31]

"Why We Won the Deal" Kudos Memo

The "Why We Won the Deal" memo is a powerful tool to not only analyze your success but also celebrate it. It offers a platform to appreciate the efforts of the team and highlight the tactics that worked, fostering a culture of recognition and mutual learning.

After the successful closure of a deal, the salesperson can write a memo outlining the key factors that led to the victory. This should include a brief description of the client's problem, our proposed solution, and how we convinced the client that our solution is the best fit for their needs.

---

30   Farrokh, A., & Cegelski, N. (2023). *Cold Calling Sucks (and That's Why It Works)*. 30 MPC.

31   Blount, J. (2015). *Fanatical Prospecting: The Ultimate Guide to Opening Sales Conversations and Filling the Pipeline by Leveraging Social Selling, Telephone, Email, Text, and Cold Calling*. Wiley.

This memo is not solely for encouragement; it serves as a learning tool for the team, demonstrating effective strategies and offering insights that others can apply in their sales pursuits. Moreover, this practice of writing a "Why We Won the Deal" memo instills a culture of reflection and continuous learning. It insists on the importance of understanding our success, not just celebrating it.

However, perhaps the most important aspect of this memo is the recognition it brings to the team members. It's an opportunity to highlight the contributions of each individual and give credit where it's due. This practice enhances team morale and motivates members to strive for success in future deals.

In essence, the "Why We Won the Deal" memo is a testament to our team's capabilities, a tool for learning and improvement, and a celebration of our collective success.

CONCLUSION

If one is illuminated, are not all illuminated? - **Ra**

The IGST Framework is more than just a collection of techniques. It's a philosophy that emphasizes the interconnectedness of your **Intention**, the driving force behind your actions, your **Goals**, the specific targets you aim to achieve, the **Strategies**, the grand plans that guide your journey, and the **Tactics**, the concrete actions that bring those plans to life. In other words, it is a dynamic journey of continuous learning and growth.

By aligning these elements, you create a harmonious symphony that propels you towards your goals. Just as a skilled musician understands the relationship between notes, chords, and instruments, mastering the IGST Framework equips you to orchestrate your own path to success.

As I mentioned previously, the last few years were very difficult personally, but I felt as though I was being carried forward by the momentum this system creates in life. The energy and intention placed on my successful realization of my goals has carried me when I was going through the lowest times of life.

To quote Neville Goddard, "There is an enormous difference between attention directed objectively and attention directed subjective, and the capacity to change your future depends on the latter."[32]

Your **Intention** serves as the seed of your imagination, and through the IGST Framework, you cultivate that seed into a flourishing reality. By aligning your strategies and tactics with your clear intention, you empower your imagination to shape your world into your desire and achieve your full potential. As you encounter new challenges and opportunities, revisit and refine your framework, adapting it to your evolving goals and aspirations. This iterative process ensures that your personal operating system remains effective and responsive to changing circumstances, empowering you to achieve sustained high performance.

I hope you can apply this operating system in a meaningful way. It's entirely changed my life, and I hope it changes yours, too.

Dream big.

---

32   Goddard, N. (1954). *The Power of Awareness*. DeVorss & Company

Made in the USA
Monee, IL
29 September 2024